I0708914

COSCOM
ENTERTAINMENT

Also by A.P. Fuchs

Blood of My World Trilogy

Discovery of Death
Memories of Death
Life of Death

Undead World Trilogy

Blood of the Dead
Possession of the Dead
Redemption of the Dead

The Axiom-man™ Saga
(listed in reading order)

Axiom-man
Episode No. 0: First Night Out
Doorway of Darkness
Episode No. 1: The Dead Land
City of Ruin
Episode No. 2: Underground Crusade
Outlaw
Of Magic and Men (comic book)

Mech Apocalypse

Mech Apocalypse

Other Fiction

A Stranger Dead
A Red Dark Night
April (writing as Peter Fox)
Magic Man (deluxe chapbook)
The Way of the Fog (The Ark of Light Vol. 1)
Devil's Playground (written with Keith Gouveia)
On Hell's Wings (written with Keith Gouveia)
Zombie Fight Night: Battles of the Dead
Magic Man Plus 15 Tales of Terror
Undeniable

ANTHOLOGIES (AS EDITOR)

DEAD SCIENCE
ELEMENTS OF THE FANTASTIC
VICIOUS VERSES AND REANIMATED RHYMES: ZANY ZOMBIE POETRY FOR THE UNDEAD HEAD
METAHUMANS VS THE UNDEAD
BIGFOOT TERROR TALES VOL. 1 (WITH ERIC S. BROWN)
BIGFOOT TERROR TALES VOL. 2 (WITH ERIC S. BROWN)
METAHUMANS VS WEREWOLVES

NON-FICTION

BOOK MARKETING FOR THE FINANCIALLY-CHALLENGED AUTHOR
CANADIAN SCRIBBLER: COLLECTED LETTERS OF AN UNDERGROUND WRITER
LOOK, UP ON THE SCREEN! THE BIG BOOK OF SUPERHERO MOVIE REVIEWS
GETTING DOWN AND DIGITAL: HOW TO SELF-PUBLISH YOUR BOOK
THE CANISTER X TRANSMISSION: YEAR ONE

POETRY

THE HAND I'VE BEEN DEALT
HAUNTED MELODIES AND OTHER DARK POEMS
STILL ABOUT A GIRL

GO TO
WWW.CANISTERX.COM

the

canister x transmission

year one

collected newsletters from

may 10, 2014 – may 2, 2015

by

a.p. fuchs

COSCOM ENTERTAINMENT
WINNIPEG

ISBN 978-1-927339-55-8

Published by COSCOM ENTERTAINMENT

A.P. FUCHS website: www.canisterx.com

Text set in Garamond; Printed and Bound in the USA

COVER DESIGN BY A.P. FUCHS

This is for all the readers who care about what they're favorite creators are doing, and this is for the creators who care about what they're readers are reading.

the
canister X
transmission

year one

Issue Zero - June 19, 2015

Welcome to the first collection of *The Canister X Transmission* newsletters. Within are Issues 1 through 52 of the weekly newsletter. Year One, in short.

As promised, this is Issue 0, a newsletter exclusive to this collection and not available anywhere else.

I hope it serves as an intro to the collection to follow.

And if you've bought this collection but haven't signed up for the free weekly newsletter, please do so at www.tinyletter.com/apfuchs

So . . . a breakdown of each section.

0.1

Every newsletter was opened with a creative thought of the week. The longer I spent in this business, the more I found myself theorizing about books and comics, both in terms of the art forms themselves and in terms of how I approach and execute them. Of course, throughout the years, my opinions and ideas on both have changed and still continue to evolve, which speaks of art's ability and capability to be an almost living thing.

Sharing the creative thought of the week with you was always a highlight because it was a chance to express what was going on in my head about a particular issue and was a means to bounce it off people other than myself. To be able to either give an opinion about something or a how-to was rewarding because one of the things that drive me as an author is to not see others make the same mistakes I did in the beginning of my career. These thoughts were also shared as a point of comfort for other writers and artists in the context of being someone they can relate to, someone who was also mulling over strange ideas about writing and creating. Perhaps, even, someone who had the same ideas.

One of my favorite things to do is talk shop with other creators. It's satisfying to share to my experiences with them and to hear their thoughts on the creative process. I've also been able to learn from them and test out their methods to see if they're a fit for me. Sometimes they were, sometimes they weren't, but growth is everything and the longer you keep at this, the more steps you'll be taking forward than backward if you keeping trying new things and being open to suggestions.

In the end, I'm pleased with the topics that came out over the course of Year One and have carried over the creative thought of the week in a similar manner into Year Two.

At the very least, thanks for listening to this crumudgeon of a writer blab week-to-week whether you agreed with him or not.

Writing's about honest expression, win, lose or draw.

0.2

Work updates are important, I think, between the reader and writer. Constant work updates—i.e. daily—are a pain, but a weekly "Here's what's going on," I think, is a good thing and helps get folks excited about what you're producing. It also makes the writer accountable to their audience because if they say they're working on something and it has to be done by such and such a date, then they better deliver. (Note: I haven't always been good at that, but I try.) Likewise, since—so far as I was aware—most of the Year One newsletter receivers were creators themselves, giving behind-the-scenes info was always a plus because I personally love hearing about what my favorite creators are working on and when I could possibly buy the finished project.

It also keeps me motivated, both telling you what I'm doing and hearing what others are doing.

And motivation is good in a business that can sometimes suck you dry.

0.3

I'm a huge loser and I'm proud to say it. I love all sorts of geekdom, with an ultra soft spot for superheroes. The third section of the newsletter was a chance to talk about what was going on in the world of fandom during the week and highlight an item of interest that might also appeal to the nerds on the list. (And being a nerd is a good thing; we make the world go round.)

I can talk about superheroes for hours, so sometimes compressing my nerd news item of the week was tough, but I think I pulled it off.

However, I do admit this regular third section of the newsletter didn't 100% fit in with the rest of it, which was about writing and publishing books.

Meh.

It was fun.

And I'm still a dork.

0.4

In the interest of being transparent, I admit section four was meant to be a kind of selling feature for the newsletter. I needed to offer something of value to get people to sign up so closing off each issue with a publishing or marketing tip was my way of duping you into signing up. It paid off, so thanks. *wink wink*

But I'm glad I got to pass onto you things I've learned about selling your books and comics over the years and perhaps saved you some trials of your own. This fourth section was also a way for me to get my thoughts out on paper about those subjects and, maybe one day, expand and collect them in book format as a sister guide to my how-to self-publishing book, *Getting Down and Digital: How to Self-publish Your Book*.

For those who've read Year One already, I hope you found the items introduced helpful, and if you're going to read them here for the first time, I hope they give you a boost and offer insight into some of the dos and don'ts of book and comic marketing.

With the above said, it's time to sign off and let you get reading.

I really love this newsletter as a form of communication. Hope you like it, too.

Disclaimer: Please note the newsletters within are reprinted here as they had been originally sent out save for a little formatting for aesthetics. If you find any typos, don't worry, other people got them first.

Thanks.

- A.P. Fuchs
Winnipeg, MB

End transmission.

Issue 1 - May 10, 2014

Welcome to the first issue of *The Canister X Transmission.*

First, thanks for subscribing to this newsletter. I hope to amuse, entertain and inform you throughout its duration.

1.1

One of the things I want to include are musings on the creative life. It sounds extremely pretentious to even say that. I mean, “creative life” sounds terrible, but it’s the only way to sum it up.

It’s not all sunshine and rainbows either so my comments on it will be about the good side of it and the bad side. It’s going to be about transparency.

This week, let’s focus on the good: being your own boss. Whether you’re a fulltime artist or not, when it comes time to getting the work done, you are your own boss. You tuck yourself away in your little corner and create for hours on end, answering to no one but yourself. The people you have to answer to are either those you are turning your project in to or your readers.

In my case, it’s my readers. I set my own schedule, but if I promise a book in a certain timeframe, I need to make sure I deliver it so have to keep how many hours I need to complete the task in mind. The good news is I can start when I want, end when I want, take breaks when I want or need them. Can’t do that at a regular job. It also commands a great deal of discipline because the work doesn’t get done by itself. But to sit there, write for a bit, feel the muse leave then go for a break when the mood strikes? It’s precious and it’s one of the reasons I wanted to work for myself for many years.

I like doing things and I like getting things done, whether that’s writing or otherwise, but I’m very much a my-own-schedule kind of man. Not sure if that’s to do with having an issue with authority or not. I just like being left to my own devices and am able to produce if left alone. I tend to get frustrated when I know I have to produce on someone else’s clock.

Maybe I'm the only one like that or maybe there are others, I don't know, as I know some people revel in having a schedule. I'm not all over the place, mind you, but my motto has always been that as long as the work gets done by a certain time, you should be able to approach it at your own pace.

My feelings on this are probably partly fueled by my being fed up with the rat race of modern society and its insane need to go-go-go.

No thanks.

Let me just write and let me get it done, but don't breathe down my neck about it.

1.2

In fanboy news, I learned that DC Comics is canceling *Nightwing* after the 30th issue, which is a shame as it was really getting good. Issues 28 and 29 were awesome and I was eager to see where the story would go with issue 30. Guess it doesn't matter now because, I mean, they got one issue to wrap up everything. Something tells me it's going to be rushed.

Also obsessed with daily searching Twitter for new *Batman vs Superman* news. Sometimes I find something, sometimes not, but, of course, I'm after leaked photos or inside information. Really looking forward to the costume reveals, but that most likely won't happen until summer around Comic Con at the earliest. The movie's two long years away yet so they can't just dump a bunch of stuff on the public this early in the game.

Needless to say, I'm very excited. The only thing I don't get is why Batman is getting top billing in this *Man of Steel* sequel. Shouldn't it be *Superman vs Batman* instead?

1.3

Work continues on Secret Project No. 1. As of this writing, I'm about 28,400 words into it (I'm writing this the 6th). I estimate it to be around 50,000 words when done, maybe 55. We'll see when we get there. If I hit 60,000, that's fine, too, but I don't really want to go higher. The main thing about these books is they're supposed to be quick-paced, loads of action, and shorter reads.

1.4

Publishing tip: I'll say it again in this first issue because it's so, so important—research. Research, research, research, whether you're wanting to publishing traditionally or independently. Do your research, find out what tools you'll need to achieve your goal, and then go about the task. I've already traveled the road of just jumping in and have paid many high prices over the years as a result. For publishing, get your information ducks all lined up in a row and then go about the task, especially if it's your first time out. You'll thank yourself later.

For an in-depth, step-by-step self-publishing guide, go here to download my book, *Getting Down and Digital: How to Self-publish Your Book*. No hype. Just pure, honest self-publishing. http://amzn.to/1eBljN5

Thanks for tuning in to the first issue of *The Canister X Transmission*. I hope you enjoyed it. Issue two coming next Saturday.

Until next time, I can be found on the web at canisterx.com , facebook.com/apfuchsbooks and twitter.com/ap_fuchs

End transmission.

Issue 2 - May 17, 2014

Welcome to the second issue of *The Canister X Transmission*. If you know of anyone else who would be interested in subscribing for free, please pass them this link: www.tinyletter.com/apfuchs

2.1

Last week we talked about one of the good sides to writing and creating and that was being your own boss.

This week I wanted to touch on one of the downsides: the loneliness.

Writing is a solitary job with long hours spent by yourself living in the worlds you create. Sure, you have your characters to keep you company, but in terms of real-world contact, unless you're one of those people who can work while others are in the same room, you're on your own. It's not too bad for short stretches, but when you've got the day by yourself—lately I've been finding the need to be around others. As of this writing, I'm home alone during the day while the Mrs. is at work and the boys are at school. The loneliness is getting to me. Could be because I'm at a vulnerable point in my life right now and need human contact. I'll often get on the phone several times a day and talk to others to try and bridge the gap until the boys get home.

At the same time, I need the alone time because I can't write with others in the room. I need to concentrate, especially if I'm at a part in the novel that requires intense thought (i.e. an action scene or major plot details).

I'm sure I'm not the only writer who struggles with this.

2.2

I write this on the 13th and today they revealed Ben Affleck as Batman along with the new batmobile. He looks amazing. I mean, seriously amazing. The suit is classic Batman, no armor, and they used the same stuff they used for the *Man of Steel* suit that made it look like Superman's muscles were flexed all the time. I was hoping they would use a similar material for the Batsuit and it looks like they have. I'm a Ben Affleck fan so between the suit and how much I like him as an actor, I know this new incarnation of Batman is going to be the best yet.

The batmobile also looks incredible, a cross between the tumbler from the Christopher Nolan films and the Michael Keaton mobile. They didn't make it over the top in either direction thus grounding it in reality as much as possible. Can't wait to see it in action.

2.3

Secret Project No. 1 is about 11,000 words from completion as of this writing. My hope—assuming my 50,000-word final word count was accurate—is to finish it by the 19th. Then I'll probably take a day or two break and get on with Secret Project No. 2. The plan is to write Secret Projects Nos. 1-3 first then go back and do the edits for each.

2.4

Publishing tip: getting the work done. I procrastinate now and then, too, but I know that books don't get written just thinking about them. You need to actually sit down and write and get it done. It's easy to put it off and come up with excuses like "I'm tired," or "The muse isn't there," or "I'm just not feeling it right now," but the reality is those excuses are usually overridden by simply sitting down at the computer and writing. It's like writer's block. It only happened to me once on my first book, but upon looking back, I no longer believe in it. To be so blocked that you can't write a single thing? I'm sorry, all it takes is the act of sitting down and picking up where you left off. Sure, the scene might not be the most amazing thing ever, but—to me, anyway—the writing stage isn't the best time to assess that because you read and write at different rates. I can't tell you how many times I've written something and wasn't completely happy only to go back during the rewrite phase and find out I did a good job after all.

The tip this week is to get the work done. To set aside the time, to *make* the time if you need to and just simply do it. That's part of being a writer. You're only a writer if you write.

If you've already done the work and are looking for a simple, step-by-step self-publishing guide, my book, *Getting Down and Digital: How to Self-publish Your Book*, is available for download here: http://amzn.to/1eBljN5

Like I mentioned last time, I can be found on the web at canisterx.com , facebook.com/apfuchsbooks and twitter.com/ap_fuchs

End transmission.

Issue 3 - May 24, 2014

Welcome to the third issue of *The Canister X Transmission.* If you know of anyone else who would be interested in subscribing for free, please pass them this link: www.tinyletter.com/apfuchs

3.1

Mission accomplished. That's the side of writing I really love: when you finish writing your book. I finished Secret Project No. 1 yesterday—the 19th—and before composing this newsletter wrote the first draft synopsis for it.

The sense of accomplishment of finishing a book still feels good lo these many books later. Some might think I'd just go, "Meh, finished another one," and move on, but for me, it's still a thrill. It's also a relief. Not in a bad way, but while I'm in the middle of a writing project, my head feels full as it works out the plot details, thinks of new scenes, struggles with—sometimes—what to write next. Now all that's over with because the book is done so there's a peace that comes with finishing a book.

I also get excited because I know that down the line I'll have to go back for rewrites and will get to read the book as a whole. You see, you read and write at different speeds so to go back and read the book as one giant unit versus chunk by chunk puts a new spin on it, and it's that spin that ultimately the reader gets to experience.

So right now I'm feeling good, feeling relieved, and getting geared up to write Secret Project No. 2, which I hope to start this week.

3.2

DC Universe On-line is my PS3 game of choice and has been for years. I'll take breaks from it now and then—like to play the new Batman *Arkham* games when they come out—but I always go back to *DCUO*. I play as Axiom-man ("Axiomman" in the game as they don't allow hyphens) so if you want to look me up, search that handle. My character's costume changes, but I also play as Axiom-man dressed in his uniform as depicted on the book covers. Well, a very close version as the *DCUO* costume options doesn't make for an exact match. Still really cool to see one's own character in "live action" like that.

As part of one of their recent game updates, they streamlined the currency again, which means that I don't have to play just the harder levels to level up my character. I can play some of the easier ones as well. Of course, the easier ones don't reward you as big as the hard ones at the stage I'm at—working on getting my first piece of T5 armor—but it still means I can get there if I play long enough.

The game is amazing and truly covers the DC Universe. I'm sure I'll talk about it more in future newsletters so will end this segment off by saying the game covers both the open worlds of Metropolis, Gotham, the Watchtower (Hall of Doom, if you play as a villain), as well as separate levels (i.e. Oa, Central City and others).

It's an amazing game and I can't wait to see how it looks once I finally upgrade to a PS4.

3.3

As mentioned, the first draft to Secret Project No. 1 was completed yesterday. Now it's on to Secret Project No. 2. The story picks up right where the first one left off and the overall arc will finally end in Secret Project No. 3.

What are these secret projects I keep talking about? Stay tuned as I will make title announcements soon enough.

3.4

Here's your publishing tip of the week (and please note I'm doing these at random): use both the on- and off-line worlds. There's so much stuff going on about eBooks this and eBooks that that so many writers seem to be forgetting there's a whole world of books that exist off the computer screen or eReader. You need to not only have your book as an eBook, but also as a paperback—even a hardcover, if you choose—so you could sell your book off-line as well.

Where? Do book signings, convention sales, trunk-of-car sales to family, friends, co-workers, even perfect strangers. A lot of people still read physical books and if you can get yours in front of them by physically selling it to them, you're doing yourself and your career a major service. The on-line marketing place is so painfully crowded right now, but the off-line marketplace isn't nearly as bad for the savvy book marketer. I don't see 200,000 authors all crowded into my local bookshop shouting "Buy my book!" like I do on-line. You could be the only voice there if you set up a signing.

For more in-depth publishing info and a step-by-step guide, please see my book, *Getting Down and Digital: How to Self-publish Your Book*, available for download here: http://amzn.to/1eBljN5

Likewise, I can be found elsewhere on the web at canisterx.com , facebook.com/apfuchsbooks and twitter.com/ap_fuchs

End transmission.

Issue 4 - May 31, 2014

Here we are, already at the fourth issue of *The Canister X Transmission.* Time's flying.

Welcome.

4.1

Been thinking about writing routines lately. Every writer has one, so far as I know. This is different from a writer's "process" (that sounds so pretentious). The process is *how* they write; the routine is what they *do* to write.

Lately I've gone back to the routine I had for years. I started smoking again after being clean for over a year—long story; I plan on quitting soon—so my current routine is the one I used to write numerous books with in the past. It's basically me turning on the laptop and booting up MSWord, grabbing my coffee and going outside for a smoke to mull over the next scene in my head, then going back in and writing down what I thought about outside. Right now, I can't just turn on the computer and go. I mean, I'm sure I could if I really wanted to—I kind of did that during the time I had quit smoking—but right now I'm in a place where I need to go step-by-step with things and that's how I view the routine. Step one: turn on computer. Step two: smoke and think. Step three: go back in and write. Then when I'm done, I'm done. I'm always saving as I'm typing, but when I finish my session for the day, I update the file on the USB drive so I have a copy just in case something screwy happens.

That's my routine. Feel free to email me and tell me yours. I enjoy hearing what other writers and artists do.

4.2

They recently announced the official title to *Batman vs Superman,* which is *Batman v. Superman: Dawn of Justice.* Personally, I like it. Like every other comic book fan on the planet, I wanted them to title it *World's Finest*, but I'm still happy with their choice. Clearly they're building something and "Dawn of Justice" indicates, well, the beginning of the Justice League.

Rumor has it *Batman v. Superman* is shooting back-to-back with *Justice League* so the word choice makes sense.

I foresee this movie laying the groundwork for a JLA one, with the ending somehow indicating they're going to need a team to handle whatever's coming next. I also suspect we'll get a glimpse of whatever's happening next at the end of the flick because the rumor mill also said DC and Warner Bros. plan on cliffhanging their movies as their signature move as opposed to adding a bonus scene(s) like Marvel does. I also heard they plan on doing short films at the end of each feature to further set them apart from the competition.

Only time will tell.

4.3

According to my word-o-meter at www.canisterx.com, Secret Project No. 2 is sitting at 24% complete as of this writing. Good progress. That's about a quarter finished. I'm very much taking this book scene-by-scene as that's how the ideas are coming right now. I have a super vague idea of the overall story, but it's so loose that I haven't committed to it fully. Since I believe stories tell themselves, I'm just seeing where this one goes.

4.4

Publishing tip of the week:

Get an accountant. There's a business side to all this and if you foresee your financial items being more complicated than simple money-in/money-out, then I suggest hiring a bookkeeper or an accountant to help you keep things straight. In fact, I'd talk to one right at the beginning of your venture—or at the beginning of your tax year—to help give you an idea of how to keep things as simple as possible. The last thing you want is to have all your time and mental energy taken up by the financial logistics of selling books instead of actually writing and marketing them. It's totally worth the fee for a consultation as it'll save you a headache and precious time later.

Speaking from experience. I only recently hired a bookkeeper and already she's been an enormous help in aiding me in streamlining all that I got going on over here.

Really awesome.

That's it for this week. Remember, I'm also on the web at canisterx.com , facebook.com/apfuchsbooks and twitter.com/ap_fuchs

End transmission.

Issue 5 - June 7, 2014

Welcome to Issue Five of *The Canister X Transmission.*

5.1

Writing in bulk. That's what I'm doing right now: writing Secret Projects Nos. 1-3 all at once and then releasing them instead of just going one by one. I've only done this one other time before, and that was with the *Blood of my World* Trilogy, a series of novellas. Secret Projects 1-3 will be about double that length when done.

Why am I doing this when it would certainly be easier to release them one at a time? I'm playing with marketing. I was talking to a fellow writer the other week and he said that people want series books now and they want them all available. Makes sense. It's tough to sometimes wait between each installment in your favorite series. I'm hoping that by releasing these three projects all at once there will be a sales payoff in the end. Not that money is the motivator. Part of it is scheduling, and the last time I finished a trilogy—the *Undead World Trilogy*—it was two years between each installment. For *The Axiom-man Saga,* I'm kind of on a weird schedule with that. I released one book in 2006, two in 2007, one in 2008, then one in 2012 and two in 2013. I'm hoping for at least one this year, maybe two. That, and since the next Axiom-man story arc is a four-parter, I need to have my head clear of other ideas so I can just focus solely on him hence why I'm doing Secret Projects 1-3 all in a row. Sort of a "get them done and out of my head" kind of thing.

Is this the better way to write? I don't know. For a series, it seems to work better for me to do it in bulk because Secret Projects 1-3 is a trilogy that makes up one giant story. By doing all three, I get to live in the world of all three and compose it as a whole instead of part one, release, part two, release, etc. It also enables me to go back and make changes to, say, book one if the stories of books two or three merit it. Once something's published, it's done and going back to change something would be a headache and a half.

From a sales perspective, only time will tell.

My marketing experience with the *Blood of my World Trilogy*, having them all available at once, didn't pan out, but it did feel good to have three books to present to market and add to my backlist.

I'm also playing with a new genre with the Secret Projects so am trying not to think about the marketing of the series too much and just focus on the writing of it and devote all my mental energy there.

I'm also one of the few writers who doesn't obsess over sales either as I lost the "money as a driving force in this business" mentality a long time ago. Money as a motivator, to me, is empty and meaningless. It's nice to make sales, sure, but I stopped making them my be all and end all.

5.2

In fanboy news, I found out today—the 3rd—that *Batman: Arkham Knight*, the latest game in the *Batman Arkham* video game franchise, has been moved to 2015 instead of this fall as planned. Fine by me considering the game wouldn't be coming out for PS3 anyway so that buys me more time to save up for a PS4. I haven't decided when I'm going to upgrade my system. Right now they're around $450. Pretty pricey. Hoping they'll come down by this time next year, then I can buy one. Besides, I want my widescreen TV first. Still don't have one of those.

5.3

Work has slowed on Secret Project No. 2. I took several days off last week to let my head rest and the production this week has been about half output thus far.

I'm going through a tough season mentally in that I don't seem to have much mental energy available due to some other factors—i.e. the business end of publishing. I'm hoping to remedy this soon, though I don't think I'll make my end-of-June deadline for the completion of Secret Project No. 3

5.4

This week's publishing tip is automation, namely Twitter and Facebook.

It's easy to get stuck in the social media vortex and spend a lot of time there, not only socializing but promoting one's work. I use Hootsuite. It's free and I can preprogram it to send out automated tweets or Facebook messages for whenever I want. This then frees me up to use social media to just socialize instead of always promoting. It doesn't take long to preprogram, especially if you have all your tweets in a Word doc ahead of time. I load it up for the month and then I don't have to think about it.

It's recommended if you're looking to save some promo time.

Go to www.hootsuite.com

Anyway, that's it for now.

You can find me elsewhere on the web at canisterx.com , facebook.com/apfuchsbooks and twitter.com/ap_fuchs

End Transmission

Issue Six - June 11, 2014

Welcome to Issue Six of *The Canister X Transmission.* This week's newsletter is coming to you early.

6.1

We've been talking a bit about writing methods, so today I wanted to tackle another one: pantsing versus plotting, or a combination thereof. Those are the only three ways to write a manuscript so far as I know. Feel free to send me a note telling me of another one.

In case you're new to the terms, "pantsing" means you write your book by the seat of your pants. You don't plan anything, you just write and see where the story takes you. "Plotting"—also called "outlining"—is when you plot out the details of your book either scene-by-scene or chapter-by-chapter. In other words, you construct a roadmap of what-happens-when before writing your book.

And, of course, you can do a combo of the above.

For me, I've always been a pantser. When I sat down to write my first book, I actually intended to write a series of short stories that would all link together. Instead, I realized I had the makings of a much longer story and thus kept writing to see where the story would take me.

I still do that. I have an idea for a story, then I get an idea for an opening scene and away I go. To me, I find it a more honest way to write in that I let the story dictate what happens versus me dictating what happens. The most I do in terms of "plotting" is I might get an idea for a later scene and I'll write a few sentences about it at the end of my manuscript then delete the note once I get to it. Otherwise, yeah, I let the story tell itself. It's more organic that way. Plus, my opinion on it is it's a more creative way to write because if I wrote down what happens ahead of time, I kind of need to keep things that way in order to get from A-Z. If Point G changes, it'll affect Point H then Point I and so on down the line. I might end up replotting the whole thing. At least with pantsing, I can let the creativity flow, and if the story takes a twist, I can just roll with it without fear of it "upsetting my plan."

As well, the other kind of "plotting" I do is simply getting a general idea of where the story might be headed, but I don't lock it down, as in, "it has to be this way." I allow room for the story to take me in a new direction if needs be. It's happened where I thought a book would go a certain way and, well, what do you know? The story changed things on me and thus the book changed, too.

What about you? How do you write? Feel free to email me to let me know.

6.2

For a long time I've been referring to these "secret projects" I've been working on. As a newsletter subscriber, I'm revealing the titles to Secret Projects Nos. 1-3 to you first.

Ready?

The first book is called *Mechapocalypse*, a sci-fi about giant mech battles and exo-suited warriors amongst other things. There's loads of action, and it follows a group of four main characters.

I haven't decided if I'm going to keep the title as one word or break it into two. As it stands in the manuscripts right now, it's one word.

The next two books are called *Mechapocalypse 2* and *Mechapocalypse 3*. I might add a subtitle to each, I might not. Personally, I'm a fan of numbered series titles and I've never done it before with my books so it'll be a first for me. Might as well.

I already have some ideas about cover art and title design. I look forward to sharing them with everybody when the time comes.

6.3

I feel like the worst fanboy ever. I still haven't seen *Captain America: The Winter Soldier* or *The Amazing Spider-Man 2*.

No real excuse other than it's my being a parent that's holding me back.

I'm not complaining, to be clear, but long gone are the days the wife and I can just up and go to a movie. Now we need to arrange a sitter and, for us, they're in short supply.

Normally, because it's superheroes, I'd just take my kids to go see the movies, but ever since learning our lesson with *Iron Man 3*, we pre-screen super flicks from now on. Those Extremis guys in *IM3* scared my kids big time.

Never again.

I just hope I can catch *Cap 2* and *Spidey 2* at the cheapies before they leave the big screen.

6.4

I'm a big fan of off-line sales in today's on-line-sales-focused publishing climate. I suppose it's partly because I tend to do better off-line than I do on-line, one of the reasons being the on-line marketplace is so painfully crowded right now.

Business cards. Have them. Give them out. Not everyone does and a business card is your way of handing a ticket to someone to find out what you're all about. Not only should it include doors into your on-line world—website, Twitter, Facebook, email address, etc.—but it also serves as a door to your off-line world by being a reminder as to who you are. You have your name, then beneath it, instead of just putting "author" or "writer"—which are fine—you can take it a step further and put "sci-fi author" or "romance novelist" or something. An identifier of some sort.

To further dress up your card, you can customize them by including your book or graphic novel's cover. By putting your product on the card, it immediately forms a connection in the receiver's mind what you are about and what you've done. That way, later, if they didn't get a book from you right away, they have this point of reference and can take that card to the store and have someone look up the book or pull it off the shelf.

Business cards are dual-sided, too, so unlike on-line adverts where all the info needs to be in your face in one location, you can divide up your card into two by having, say, all your contact details, etc. on the front, and images of your book covers on the back along with ISBN data and where they can be purchased.

Last, you can either design your card to double as a bookmark or design your bookmark to double as a business card. There are no hard and fast rules about this, so be creative.

For me, I'm almost out of my current batch of business cards—I always have them out at signings and conventions—so when it comes time for reordering, I plan on trying something new.

Hey, even writing these few paragraphs on them gave me some ideas.

Time to play around.

For more in-depth publishing info and a step-by-step guide, please see my book, *Getting Down and Digital: How to Self-publish Your Book*, available for download here: http://amzn.to/1eBljN5

I'm also on the web at canisterx.com , facebook.com/apfuchsbooks and twitter.com/ap_fuchs

Peace.

End Transmission

Issue Seven - June 21, 2014

Welcome to the seventh issue of *The Canister X Transmission*. We're back on schedule with the Saturday delivery after last week's early sending.

7.1

Playing in different mediums within the writing field.

I think it's important to stretch one's creative muscles and try new things. Like an artist who draws in pencil and ink, but who also does watercolor and oils, so too a writer should try writing in different disciplines.

I write fiction, non-fiction, comic books, articles and essays. I've written poetry as well as song lyrics. I even tried my hand at a screenplay once.

Writing in different mediums gets you to look at writing from different angles instead of always the same one such as writing prose. It gets your brain to think in new ways and, who knows, you might like writing, say, essays better than fiction. You never know. Might even find out you're better at it.

It also makes you a better writer to be versatile like that because you can then bring in different traits from different writing disciplines into your fiction, in turn developing your voice in a more unique way and, possibly, punching up your stories.

Anyway, food for thought.

7.2

Taking a break from *Mechapocalypse 2* and have started a comic book project. It's currently untitled, but it was really speaking to me last night—the 18th—and so I started writing the story the Harvey Pekar method. For those who don't know who Harvey Pekar is, quick, go Google him. Then go see the movie, *American Splendor*, which is about his life. He was one of the best comic book writers, in my opinion. I speak of him in the past tense because he died in 2010.

Anyway, yeah, I'm writing this comic the Harvey Pekar way and that is to basically draw the comic out in stick figures with the appropriate words, then go back later and draw the thing for real. Harvey only wrote his stories and had other artists, like the amazing R. Crumb, draw them. Right now I'm favoring that writing method versus the standard comic book script, which I've done in the past. Just more in a visual mode these days.

7.3

Got a new Superman figure for Father's Day for my Superman toy collection. This one was from the *Man of Steel* line, and it's called, "Split Cycle Superman." It's him in his regular supersuit with the ability to "tear" a motorcycle in half. I don't remember that scene from the movie, but whatever. I've wanted this particular toy since it came out because it's Superman in his regular supersuit and that's my toy collection: Superman in his traditional outfit from different toy series.

Happy I got it.

7.4

One of things I've found useful at comic book conventions and book signings is to have proper signage at my table.

I have multiple posters mounted on foamboard showcasing my various titles—basically a blow-up of the cover—some with ad words to tell people what they're about and/or to entice them to take a look.

I also have other signs in big print stating series names and how much each one is or how much if you buy all three or seven of them.

Clear pricing is another matter. Most people are shy so while they might be interested in your book, they might be hesitant to ask how much. Having a sign there saves them the trouble. Same with conventions. Nothing worse than seeing an author sitting with a stack of books and that's all. (I've done it.) Besides, it saves you the trouble of repeating the same thing to person after person.

Having posters and signage make a big deal out of your books, draws attention to them, and gives off an air of showmanship. And in this media-laden culture, a little showmanship to stand out from the crowd can go a long way, especially in a "non-showmanship" field like books.

In other words, make a display out of your table and don't just have a pile of books. Make signs, make posters, and keep them simple and legible.

If you want more in-depth publishing info and a step-by-step guide, please see, *Getting Down and Digital: How to Self-publish Your Book*, available for download here: http://amzn.to/1eBljN5

I'm also on the web at canisterx.com , facebook.com/apfuchsbooks and twitter.com/ap_fuchs

That's it for this week.

End Transmission

Issue Eight - June 28, 2014

Here we are: Issue Eight of *The Canister X Transmission.*

Having fun yet? I am. I mean, eight issues already. That's two months' worth of newsletters. Awesome.

8.1

How's it going?

It's a question that's tossed around all the time. Usually people just say, "Fine," and call it good. I'm done with that. Nowadays, if someone asks me how I'm doing, I'll give them an honest answer, good or bad. The latest thing I've been saying in response to "How are you?" is "Up and down," which pretty sums up how I'm feeling these days.

That's what I want to do this issue: set aside the writing/creative life stuff and tell you how I'm doing. Then, after you've read the issue, if you want to reply and tell me how you're doing, by all means, please do. Being human: we're all in it together.

Back in February we had a major event happen here which launched me into a downward spiral. It triggered a three-day panic attack, which was—no joke—three days of rapid heartbeat, trouble breathing, and violent shaking. The attack was so bad, it basically made me useless for those three days and I could barely function. It also later triggered some major obsessive-compulsive behaviors, only now of which I'm finally regaining control over. This event made me reassess my career as a writer and the type of books I was publishing, and ultimately led to a complete shutdown of all things Writer A.P. Fuchs.

On the path to recovery now. I've sought outside help, am on medication, and am simply taking things day-by-day. Right now I find it very hard to think about what's happening tomorrow or in a few days from now. Really need to go one step at a time. It's the only way I can keep it together without my heart speeding up and struggling to get enough air into my lungs. If there is something major that I need to do, I'm training myself to not think about it until I have to do it. I'm tired of fretting over things and obsessing over stuff. It sucks the life out of you.

But as said, on the path to recovery and things are much better now than they were. One of the major stresses has recently been lifted off my shoulders and the remaining stress will be partly dealt with this weekend (but you can bet I'm not focusing on it until then, that's for sure; I write this on the 26th).

That's being honest. That's the "down" on how I'm doing. The "up" is I'm getting a handle on things again, have restarted my writing career, and am not taking things as seriously as I did before. I still care about my work and all that, but I'm done obsessing over it. Now it's just something I do and that's it.

Been enjoying family and friend time, taking it easy and am loving each night when I get to go into bed with my wife and be nice and cozy. Something very special and protective about that. I feel at peace when I lie next to her.

What about you? How are you doing?

8.2

Recently I've had to seek income outside of the writing field so I'm a lot more tired than usual—my meds have a fatigue-inducing side effect on top of that—so haven't been as productive as of late. I feel terrible. But, day-by-day, right? Even item-by-item. Right now my goal is to finish this newsletter then check email. After that, I'm hoping to work on that graphic novel I started, but if I don't end up doing that, I'm okay with it because I wrote this newsletter and checked email. That's a win.

I have plans for that graphic novel once it's finally done. You'll see.

8.3

Apparently Aquaman is going to be in *Batman v Superman: Dawn of Justice*, to be played by Jason Momoa. What a loaded cast! Superman, Batman, Wonder Woman, Cyborg, Lex Luthor and now Aquaman. Crazy! But from what I understand, it'll be in a cameo-type role, so no big deal. Be cool to see how it all turns out. I think DC is doing some real world-building with this movie so the groundwork will be laid for when *Justice League* comes out. DC is great at universe creation—see *DC Universe Online*, for example—so I know the world presented in *Batman v Superman* will be one that *feels* like a real universe once all is said and done.

I'm obsessed with following the production of this movie. Rumor has it some footage will be shown at Comic Con in July. Can't wait for it to leak on-line!

8.4

Publishing tip: gutters. They're important. Gutters are a bit of extra space on one side of each page. For example, on an odd-numbered page, the gutter would be on the left. For an even-numbered page, it's on the right. This extra space—a quarter inch is fine—allows for the folding of the spine and enables the reader to see all the text on the page instead of having to crack the book open 180 degrees to get it all.

Make sure your book has them when formatting. In MSWord, it's under Page Layout-Margins-Custom Margins. As mentioned, a quarter inch is fine, so type in .25 into the Gutter field and you're good. Of course make sure it's applied to the Whole Document, not just a section of it. I go over book formatting in my book, *Getting Down and Digital: How to Self-publish Your Book*, and walk you through it.

Gutters really add a level of professionalism to your finished book.

Are there any particular publishing or marketing tips you'd like to see in this newsletter? Simply reply and let me know. Likewise, if you think anyone in your circle(s) would benefit from this newsletter, feel free to forward it to them or suggest they sign up at http://www.tinyletter.com/apfuchs

Anyway, a question (and answer):

What happens when someone gives you superpowers but doesn't say what they're for? Find out in AXIOM-MAN http://amzn.to/1khtYfz

Thanks for tuning it. Catch ya next week!
End transmission.

Issue Nine - July 5, 2014

Here we go, the ninth issue of *The Canister X Transmission.*

9.1

I was on the phone the other day with my dad and I was mentioning how I was feeling discouraged with this business—hey, I'm an artist and talks like these happen now and then—and at the end of it, he said something along the lines of, "Remember the first rule of being an artist: you do it because you love it. Success and an audience are just bonuses." Frankly, I really needed to hear that because it's a reminder of the core reason I do what I do: I love doing it.

It's easy to be swept up in aspiring to be this huge commercial success, be famous, or compare oneself to other writers who seem to have it together, etc., but totally lose oneself in the process.

I remember back when I wrote my first book. At first it was going to be a series of short stories that all tied together. Soon I realized I had the makings of a novel. And so I worked on that novel for eleven months. All that mattered was the story and the need to write it all down. Sure, I had thoughts now and then about it being published and launching me into fame, but that was backburner stuff. All I was really interested in at the time was the writing of it. It was such a magical time. No pressure. No business obligations. Just me, my book and solitude. I wrote some of it on the computer, some longhand, kept notes—just lived in the world of the story.

And I was happy.

I admit I've lost some of that over the years of trying to keep up with this business, but ever since my meltdown a few months ago, I've been able to reassess my priorities and what I truly care about. One of the things that has surfaced is simply getting back to basics: write because I love it, not because of what that book might mean to me in terms of success. In the end, I should be in a place mentally to be able to write a novel, finish it, then stick it in a drawer never to be published and be totally happy with that. Why? Simply because the creation of it is what I love to do.

There's value in that.

My dad was and is onto something. The more I think about just writing something because I love it, the more I'm filled with peace and the happier I become.

I'm going to take that lesson and apply it to my current projects. I'm just going to write them and not fret about their future.

Just going to write because I love it.

9.2

There's a story idea I've been kicking around in my head for a good while and lately it's been coming to the surface. It's for a series of books on a topic of keen interest to me—a fairly popular one—but one I think I have a unique take on. While it's true I currently have other stuff on the go creatively, I'm thinking of adding this one to the mix and getting it going. I don't know how the writing of it will play into the deadlines of the others, but I also know you need to write while the ideas are loud and clear in your mind.

Something I'm mulling over, anyway. We'll see what happens, but it could be happening soon.

(I wrote the above earlier in the week. Since then I started a notebook for this series.)

9.3

Superman's my favorite superhero for a lot of reasons, but one of them is because he usually does the right thing. I look back on the Christopher Reeve movies and how he portrayed Superman as always telling the truth, upholding righteousness, and always believing in the best in people.

I want that for myself.

I think it's important we have people we look up to—*look up to*, not idolize—and, for me, it's Superman. He makes me want to be a better person, to bring a light into the dark places of this world, to stand up for the little guy, and to be known as someone who is trustworthy, dependable, and who always keeps the right thing as the most important thing in their lives.

Do I fall short? Yeah. Do I feel bad about it? Yeah. But it's the trying that means something.

Anyway, that's one of the reasons I love Superman.

He makes me want to be a better person.

9.4

Marketing tip: get a website and update it regularly.

I know for most authors, this one is obvious, but there are still authors out there who don't have a website and rely only on Facebook or Twitter or whatever to be their online presence. The thing is, you need a hub for people to check out your stuff. A website doesn't have to be anything fancy, just something that talks a bit about you, lists your books, and provides a way for readers to reach you. You can use my website, www.canisterx.com, as an example, if you wish. I use the blog format, but you don't have to. A blog is good, though, because it's an opportunity to regularly post what's going on with your books, yourself, points of interest, helpful advice, etc. It's recommended you update your blog at least once a week. Not only is this good to get readers to keep checking back, but it's also good for the search engines because they love sites that keep adding new content.

Bottom line is you need an online presence where folks can gather a bunch of information about you in one place. It's also a place to point people to when you meet them whether on-line or off-. The site basically acts as you when you're not physically there.

There are author sites I visit regularly and I know I'm not alone in this. They're an important tool to connecting with readers.

Get a website. It'll do your career good. An option would be to set up a domain and hosting with www.godaddy.com I use them and haven't had an issue. If you want to go the free route, use one of the free blog service providers like www.wordpress.com or www.blogspot.com

Thanks for tuning in this week. And now, a little commercial:

Newly endowed with superpowers, Gabriel must decide what to do with them. See him as Axiom-man in his FIRST NIGHT OUT. http://amzn.to/1fpeJPv

End transmission.

Issue Ten - July 12, 2014

Ten issues. Ten.

Welcome to *The Canister X Transmission.*

10.1

Sometimes writing can be daunting. I know I struggle with this from time to time. It's not so much the actual writing that I find hard to do, but the quantity of it. I like to set word count goals per writing session. Usually this means to write a scene from start to finish. Sometimes two. I find that, depending on what scene is next, the writing of it can sometimes appear bigger than it actually is due the estimated word count involved. In turn, this can put me off from doing it until I have the right drive, the right spark—the right *oomph*—to get it going.

Not good.

Books don't produce themselves and you need to get in the time putting one word in front of the other to get them done.

So what's the plan? Breaking the sessions into smaller chunks. Instead of doing what will probably be a 2000-word scene, why not just commit to doing only 500 words instead? 500 is better than nothing. Or, instead of writing that whole next chapter, why not just do one scene? Or in the case of a graphic novel, instead of eight pages of script, why not shoot for four?

See what I mean?

That way, you're still getting the work done.

With my schedule having changed, I need to look at alternatives to getting the books complete and breaking them down into smaller chunks seems to be the ticket right now.

10.2

Made some notes on that new series and after jotting them down and doing some research into the material I plan to tackle, I realized the project is a mammoth undertaking and, since *Mechapocalyse 2* and *3* aren't done, I'm better off finishing those first to clear up some headspace before taking on this new big project. So I've put it on the side for now and am letting my subconscious work some things out before embarking on it.

Finishing the *Mechapocalypse* books are the priority. Comic con is coming and I'd really like to have all three out by then.

10.3

Coming to a place in my wardrobe where most of my T-shirts are superhero ones. DC Comics characters, of course. I have five different Superman S shirts, two of which are from *Man of Steel.* I have a Flash logo T-shirt, a Green Lantern logo one (that glows in the dark), one with a bunch of characters on it—man, hard to find a regular shirt anymore.

Even jammie-wise I wear Superman and Batman onesies. And don't get me started on boxer shorts. I got those superhero-style, too.

Not that I'm complaining. I love them.

Just saying. Carry on.

10.4

I was thinking how writers can sometimes be shy.

This has to stop.

Whether you write fulltime or not, don't be afraid to be vocal about what you create. Tell people you're a novelist. Tell them you make comics. Most people think it's the bee's knees that you do. Admitting that you make books usually elevates you in people's eyes as to something of an expert or someone who's [above average] intelligent. Might even lead to some book sales.

It also gets word-of-mouth going. The more people mentioning you make books in conversation, the better. You never know whose itch your book might end up scratching because they heard it through the grapevine.

Okay, time to wrap it up. Thanks for tuning in, as always. Share this newsletter, tell your friends. The more the merrier. The link you can pass on for signup is www.tinyletter.com/apfuchs

Also, be sure to stop by my blog at www.canisterx.com Lots of stuff there, and also a section dedicated to self-publishing.

Cheers.

This newsletter has been brought to you by:

Axiom-man & Redsaw go head-to-head in this superhero thriller & open a doorway to an evil world DOORWAY OF DARKNESS http://amzn.to/1hMg1o1

End transmission.

Issue Eleven - July 19, 2014

This is Issue Eleven of *The Canister X Transmission.*

11.1

This is more an observation than anything else, but writers and artists are terribly underappreciated. I look at the movie and/or TV biz and it's stardom with flashing lights and fairy dust. That same actor goes out, gets mobbed, is on late-night television, goes to pop culture shows and charges an arm and a leg for autograph—on top of their [usually] enormous box office paychecks—whereas writers and artists—who do more than "act a part"—go out and are practically invisible, make way less money—sometimes next to none—and no one really seems to care about them.

Should we not be every bit as famous as actors?

Let's break it down: as said, actors simply act a part. Yes, they have to create and become the person they're portraying, but that's about as far as it goes. They're reading someone else's words and now and then improv a line or two. They wear makeup and costumes—designed by someone else—and their performance is always enhanced by music or sound effects.

I'm not trying to sell them short, but I am trying to point out something.

A writer acts out a cast of four, five, six or more characters, gives each of them their own voice, designs them both internally and externally, and decides what happens to them. This same writer also creates mood, setting, theme, sound effects, even music, and has to exercise every creative muscle to do so.

To top it all off, they have to create the story, the "what happens" to not only one person, but a multitude. We create vehicles, other-worldly devices, histories, geographies and more—all keeping track of each, mind you—in the effort to entertain.

A writer is a movie production company in one person. They play every part, every role, right from the guy holding the boom stick to the one rolling the camera to the one reading the lines.

Yet we are largely ignored by the mass media. Yes, there are writers who make headlines now and then, but compare that amount of writers to actors making headlines and you'll see an imbalance.

Frankly, I don't get it. I don't know why the term "celebrity" is typically applied to movie folks, but not to writers. When does one become famous? Is it when they've sold thousands of books? Been recognized? Been interviewed on TV, radio, etc.? Been a guest at a convention? I've done all that, yet no one cares about a writer from Canada who crafts superhero fiction.

I'm interested in hearing your thoughts. Unless it's all a visual thing and it's "people identifying so-and-so with a certain character thus they *are* that character," I'm at a loss and I think this is one of the tragedies of the creative industry as a whole.

Am I craving more personal recognition? No. I am, however, craving an appreciation for all writers do and it sucks to see us shorthanded like this.

I think if writers were treated more like their movie actor counterparts, book sales would be higher, more people would read and, dare I say, there would be a higher appreciation for the arts. It might even one day be viewed as a real vocation and not just a "dream."

Feel free to write me with your thoughts on the issue.

11.2

Got back to work on *Mechapocalypse 2*. Really happy about that. The story's mostly coming to me on a scene-by-scene basis, with vague, fog-like ideas as to where things are going/how the storyline is going to end.

Regardless, I'm enjoying getting back into it and seeing where it goes. This is my first time reading it, too, so I'm waiting to see what happens just like you guys will be once the book comes out.

11.3

Have a Superman date on Friday (I'm writing this on the 16th). My father hasn't yet seen *Man of Steel,* so he, my brother and I—possibly my brother-in-law, too—will be getting together to watch it Friday evening.

My dad's one of those closet superhero fans. He doesn't outright go geek on you when you mention a superhero, but he sees the movies and sometimes does the unexpected—like when the Death of Superman storyline hit back in the '90s. He went out and bought the black bag collector's issue. Never told me. I found out years later and thought it was the coolest thing.

Looking forward to seeing what he thinks of *Man of Steel.*

11.4

It's important to practice good writing, and I'm not just talking about when it's time to put pen to paper on whatever project you're working on. I'm talking about all the other writing you do: emails, texts, tweets, Facebook updates, honey-do lists, etc. It's about habit formation. Practice writing well in all areas of your life and it's inevitable that proper writing will make it into your fiction or comic scripts. Practice proper spelling, punctuation, grammar. These are all things that benefit you as a writer (and editor).

To me, to do otherwise is to do yourself a disservice. I mean, really, abbreviations should only be used in tweets due to the 140-character limit. Other than that, in places where there are no restrictions, go all out and do it right.

Practice makes perfect, like they say.

Something to chew on/put into effect.

Here we are, another issue done. Hope everyone is enjoying them so far. If you're just joining this newslist, you can read back issues of *The Canister X Transmission* for free at www.tinyletter.com/apfuchs under the Letter Archive.

Tell your friends about this newsletter, too, pass them the sign up link, blah blah blah . . . you know what I mean. I'm hoping to grow this list to something substantial and I thank you for coming along for the ride.

Okay. I'm done.

Enjoy your weekend.

Oh, and . . .

Suddenly sucked into a parallel world, Axiom-man finds himself fighting against the ravenous undead in THE DEAD LAND
http://amzn.to/hhuLsT

End transmission.

Issue Twelve - July 26, 2014

Here we go, the twelfth issue of *The Canister X Transmission.*

12.1

After-writing. I hyphenated the word on purpose. The after-writing sensation after finishing your word count for the day, there's nothing like it. I'm trying to think of something similar but am coming up short. For me, it's a feeling of elation and jubilation. A bit of self-pride, too. To know that my story is X amount of words closer to completion puts my mind and heart at ease in a way few things do. Personally, I find writing stress inducing. It's fun and all, but I tend to get all worked up beforehand in terms of thinking about what I'm going to write. My heart starts racing, my head feels full, and my breathing changes. As I write, I feel the pent-up story ooze out of me, the internal pressure releasing until, finally, I'm out of gas and no more words come out. That's when the after-writing—or is it after-*write*?—kicks in and I'm in a state where if for whatever reason I never wrote again, I'd be personally satisfied because I wrote that day and got words on paper.

Of course, the cycle starts up anew as time goes on, but for those half dozen or so hours after writing I'm a content man and I feel good about myself.

After-writing. I love it.

12.2

Giving some thought to comic con in the fall. A part of me wants a breather. I've been doing it every year since 2007 and there are many stresses that go along with preparing for the show: finishing new projects, packing books, ordering stock, getting my table gear in order, costuming, administration items, signage, prepping for a weekend of work—I wouldn't mind a break and just go to the show as a nerd.

If I don't go, it takes some deadline pressure off me. But then I might regret my decision. Yet if I do decide to go, that brings about the urgency to make sure everything is done and published on time.

Will make a firm decision soon. Table space is almost booked up.

12.3

Thinking of getting cable in the fall. We've been a non-cable household since 2013 began and, frankly, I'm not missing it save for Food Network. However, in the fall the new *The Flash* TV series comes out, as does *Gotham*, two superhero shows that I could watch in addition to *Arrow*.

I know some might say, "Why not stream it on-line for free?" Well, I would, if the networks had it on their websites (which they might). I won't stream from other sites, however. I mean, I've done it, but unless it's network-sanctioned, it's stealing. Same reason I don't watch movies on-line. If I didn't pay for it, it's not mine to take. Just because it's on-line doesn't give me license to watch it.

So, yeah, cable. Fall.

But to be honest, a highlight for me—as cool as I'm sure those shows will be—will be getting Food Network again. I learned to cook off that channel and I want to learn more. I just love that stuff.

12.4

Those who know me know I'm a big off-line book sales advocate. I find I have better success in one afternoon of off-line sales than I do on-line during that same afternoon.

That said, consider trying alternative markets for selling your books. Aside from book signings and conventions—as good as those are—try something else.

Last weekend I had a table during our arts festival called The Fringe. We know the folks who run the kid's side of things and they had me out to showcase my books and entertain the youngsters. I brought the entire *Axiom-man Saga* with me and the Axiom-man costume, and had a good time. I sold books and posed in the suit. To give the kids something to do, I created a fill-in-the-blank short story they could write in and customize to their liking. This brought folks to our table and I was able to show them the stuff I write.

It was an outside-the-box way to sell books.

Do you have an arts fair? Consider finding out how to get a table there. Or what about simply getting a seller's/dealer's table in the mall or at another public venue? Have you seen anyone else sell stuff like jewelry or crafts in a public space? Why not books?

Just a thought.

The on-line marketplace is painfully crowded so to find off-line places where you don't have to compete with anyone is worth its weight in gold.

That wraps up this week. Thanks for reading.

This issue was sponsored by . . .

(hehe, well, not sponsored, but these little ads are meant to encourage you to buy my books so I can make a living.)

Anyway . . .

The city is covered in a black cloud and a new supervillain has taken over. Axiom-man battles it out in CITY OF RUIN
http://amzn.to/1gxybUM

End transmission.

Issue Thirteen - August 2, 2014

This is the thirteenth issue of *The Canister X Transmission.* Sit down, pour a coffee, and read.

13.1

Second draft.

That's what's happening next with me. I decided to stop my plans of releasing all three *Mechapocalypse* books at once and publish the first one soon. I'll then release books two and three shortly after, one at a time as well.

There's something magical about the second draft. For me, it's the chance to read the book for the first time again because, honestly, I don't remember every single thing I wrote, only blips on the radar. To go back and read the book as a whole is a thrill because you get to see how your subconscious wove everything together start to finish and kept it a coherent whole. Not a perfect whole, mind you, but story-wise it's usually just fine. Rewriting sentences, fixing spelling and grammar, adjusting dialogue and thought captions, tweaking continuity, etc. is all part of the second draft process. Thing is, you read and write at different speeds. Couple that with writing a book in, say, two thousand-word chunks, and your first draft *should* be a bit clunky. Second draft is for smoothing it all out, for being unafraid to mark that page up with red—or blue or black—and rewrite entire sections if necessary. Third draft is the polish, where you spit shine all the changes you made in draft two. After that, as is my process, it goes to the editor. Draft three is as far as I can take a manuscript pre-publication before I need a fresh set of eyes on it. Then I get it back, go through the editor's edits, then edit it once more myself. That's it. Oh, it goes to my wife after my final draft for her to simply read. If, by chance, there are still any errors, they're caught at that stage. Then the book is published and you guys get to read it.

There're different schools of thought regarding the "cool down" period of a book, that is, how you long you should wait until after writing a book until you're ready to go back to it for rewrites. In Stephen King's *On Writing,* he suggests a minimum of six weeks before editing it, where you stick the book in a drawer and leave it alone. I've done his six-week wait time. I've also waited next to no time before drafts one and two. I've come to the conclusion that you should experiment with different wait times book-to-book and find out what works for you. For me, I'd like to take a minimum of a week or two between finishing the first draft and editing it. In the case of *Mechapocalypse,* according to my blog (www.canisterx.com) I finished that book May 19, so I'm over two months distanced from it.

Regardless, there needs to be a break time between first draft and second.

The plan is to edit and publish *Mechapocalypse,* then finish writing the sequel, which brings me to . . .

13.2

I made a decision about comic con in the fall. I'm going to do it, but am going to scale things back. Instead of having three tables, I'm opting for one. Going to try to fit everything on it somehow and will have to come up with some unique book stands to make it possible.

Also going to aim to have *Mechapocalypse* as my new release instead of all three. This takes major pressure off of me and ensures good writing in the books without having to rush them. Keeps the costs down, too. I *might* have a new Axiom-man episode novella for the show, but *Mechapocalypse* is the priority.

Looking forward to going small. As part of my plan since my meltdown to simplify my life, this decision seems a good way in keeping with that. That, and I won't have to worry about regretting *not* attending.

13.3

Zack Snyder released not only a picture of Gal Gadot as Wonder Woman at the San Diego Comic Con, but he also showed a teaser trailer for *Batman v Superman: Dawn of Justice.* I saw a leaked version of the trailer online and it is crazy cool. Basically it shows an armored-up Batman taking the cover off the Bat-signal and shining it into a stormy night sky, then Superman appears through the signal, eyes aglow, before cutting to the movie's logo. Gave this fanboy chills, that's for sure.

And Gal Gadot looks *wonder*ful as Wonder Woman. I knew she'd pull it off. She's filled out, the costume is incredible—kind of a warrior princess thing with Wonder Woman's colors—and she looks like she means business. I have no doubt she'll do just fine in the role, when the time comes.

13.4

Do you use Amazon's affiliate program as part of your on-line book marketing? You should, because every time someone clicks through the link and orders your book—or anything else—you get a percentage. It's tiered, too, so the more you sell, the more extra money you'll make. It's free to sign up. I've been an Amazon affiliate for years. It doesn't make me huge cash, but every bit helps and I'm thankful for it. You can also sign up as an associate for Amazon's other sites (i.e. .ca, .co.uk), too, and increase your earnings.

If you want to support me, feel free to use the links in these newsletters or on my website when you order through Amazon.com (.ca and .co.uk affiliate links are at my website under Book and Comic Shop as well). Thanks, in advance.

Go to associates.amazon.com (or .ca, .co.uk, etc.) to sign up. Once done, you can build links at the site with your affiliate code in them. Plug those links into you web marketing platform(s) and away you go.

I use the links all the time. Even the little commercials at the end of these newsletters have them.

Speaking of which . . .

What happens when a young girl versed in kung fu takes Axiom-man on a jaunt throughout the city? Find out in UNDERGROUND CRUSADE. http://amzn.to/1m0aHL5

End transmission.

Issue Fourteen - August 9, 2014

Number fourteen. *The Canister X Transmission.*

*Note: Last week's issue arrived in your inbox a couple days late. Though it was sent out on Saturday as usual, it got caught in TinyLetter's spam filter hence the delay. I suspect it was because I included Amazon's affiliate program in the subject line. It's good they have these systems in place as, frankly, spam is a waste of both the sender's and receiver's time. It was the first time this happened and, I hope, the last time.

Onto Issue Fourteen.

This is for you.

14.1

It seems I'm one of those guys who's one step behind everyone else when it comes to figuring out things about life. Or, maybe, everyone has a better poker face than me and we're all figuring things out at more or less the same time. Regardless, I tend to be one of those nuts-and-bolts types of people, the kind who needs to be shown something from the ground up so I can get a handle on it.

This kind of nuts-and-bolts approach to life transferred over to my publishing. Long ago, I thought there was a set way for writers to write a book. A set way for editing. A set way for publishing.

Even down to location of writing or editing.

I used to write at the computer. Granted, the desktop was the only one I had at the time, but it was there I started. Then I realized writing is mobile so I wrote bits of my first book longhand at coffee shops or wherever. Still typed that stuff up on the desktop, though.

For editing, I thought you needed to use a red pen because, if I remember right, I read somewhere Stephen King used a red pen and, as per years of grade school, red pen was meant for correcting mistakes. I used to sit and edit after printing out my book, hole-punching it, and sticking it in a binder.

As the years went on, I started to become mobile with my editing and edited wherever. My favorite place is in bed. I think I started this years ago when I lived in an apartment. That, and I used to do a lot of reading while lying down and since editing is similar to reading in terms of "just reading your story and checking for mistakes," I gravitated to a prone editing position.

It's now where I edit: in bed, pillows propped. I find sitting and editing too formal now. Even changed the color of my ink: blue, black, red. Whatever I have.

Here's the point: if you're a nuts-and-bolts person like me, understand that a lot of what gets a book from conception to publication is discovering what works for you and running with it. There's no set way. You can write anywhere, you can edit anywhere, you can even publish anywhere if it suits you and you have the tools needed on hand. All that matters is that, ultimately, a published book comes out of the whole thing.

As for me, I'm going to edit *Mechapocalypse.* In bed, pillows propped.

14.2

This newsletter is my new writing love. As much as I enjoy writing fiction, right now I'm big on this newsletter and earlier today—the 6th—I was thinking about how a newsletter is the perfect form of literary communication in this day and age of visual stimulation and quick quips on social media.

The art of letter writing is lost—for the most part—these days. Sure, we have email, but I know mine—both incoming and outgoing—can quickly degenerate into "Here, check this out," or "This reminded me of you," types of emails. Or, worse, email conversation where you type a sentence or two back and forth with someone. The days of sitting down and writing a well-thought-out letter to someone are past.

That's where this newsletter comes in. While it uses email as its delivery vehicle, each one is typed with a purpose, with words of intent, and is sent with the hope that what I write edifies the reader.

I can't turn this newsletter into a conversation piece because there's a decent chunk of you so one-on-one yakking back and forth is out. I also don't want them to become some informal infomercial for something either. Instead, I want these to be a mass letter to those who either care about me and my work, or care about the contents of each letter.

I hope you've been enjoying them.

For more, I wrote a blog entry on the fun I'm having writing this newsletter at: http://canisterx.com/having-fun-writing-a-newsletter

14.3

Finally saw *The Amazing Spider-Man 2* last night. Wow. What a busy movie. They crammed a lot in to a small amount of space when you think about it, however it didn't feel too crowded like it did with *Spider-Man 3*.

The good: amazing effects, especially the webslinging bits and Electro's powers. The story was solid and Peter Parker's relationship with Gwen Stacy was well done. You could feel the love those two had for each other. And Electro? Well written, especially the Max Dillon parts. I felt so bad for the guy my heart ached at his transformation scene. I also liked how it laid the groundwork for *The Sinister Six*, which is coming out in 2016.

The not-as-good: while the story was fine, it felt very convenient in terms of how things played out. Each scene, it seemed, played into the next and there was a lot of "this happened so that that could happen." Whether it was the action or the dialogue, that's the sense I got. I'm not one for convenience writing just to "move the story along."

Overall, it was a fun movie. Took the kids and the Mrs. They all liked it.

While the above isn't a thorough movie review—due to space—I do write more thought-out superhero movie reviews. Even released a book on them called *Look, Up on the Screen! The Big Book of Superhero Movie Reviews*, in which I cover 100 superhero movies. It's available here (http://amzn.to/1jVxY31) if you're interested.

14.4

Are you on Pinterest? My wife loves it as does much of our family and friends. I use it, too, and my publishing tip this week is for you to get on the Pinterest bandwagon. Why? Because the site is growing like crazy. It's photo-based and you have a pinboard on it and you can look up most any topic to find photo-related results. If you like what you see, you can "pin" it to your pinboard. You can organize your pins, too.

I'll be honest: I don't know if having a Pinterest account will actually help you sell books. However, what I do know is that by having one it adds value to your social media presence. The reason is is it gives a showcase into you as a person, the things you like, perhaps things you don't, and as a result opens you up to your readers—due to the site's photographic nature—in a way Facebook and Twitter doesn't.

I don't know about you, but for me, the more I know about a creator of something, the more apt I am to buy something of theirs. So, I suppose, in that way Pinterest can help you sell more books, that, and some of my book covers are available for pinning on Pinterest so I can pin my covers to my profile to help advertise them.

It seems writers—and other advertisers—are still trying to figure out how Pinterest fits into their overall marketing scheme, but it doesn't hurt to get in on the ground floor on one of the fastest growing social media sites on the web.

For more on Pinterest, go to www.pinterest.com

My personal Pinterest page is at www.pinterest.com/apfuchs

And speaking of marketing . . .

People are getting murdered citywide and everyone's saying the same thing: Axiom-man's gone rogue. Is it true? Find out in OUTLAW http://amzn.to/1lRfIbL

End transmission.

Issue Fifteen - August 16, 2014

Open a channel.

This is *The Canister X Transmission* Issue 15.

15.1

Vacation.

That was this past week. I took an entire week off from writing-related activities. Am even drafting up this newsletter the day of instead of earlier in the week like usual.

It's good to take a vacation from creative efforts. It's a chance to let your brain relax, relieve some stress, and just enjoy life outside of writing (or drawing).

My parents took our boys this week for their annual stay-over at Grandma and Grandpa's. For the first time in a year, the Mrs. and I had a week of evenings to ourselves to do whatever we wanted without having to bring the kids in tow. Don't get me wrong. I love my kids, but a break is nice. It's good for us so that we can have some grown up time, and it's good for the kids so they can get a new perspective on life with Mom and Dad, maybe even miss us a little bit.

We kept busy most evenings. Went to a Chinese food restaurant up on the corner that we've been meaning to go to for over a year. Went to the movies. Did some mall walking, played some video games. Was good times.

And, again, I took a break from writing stuff and let the brain recharge. Now I'm rested and ready to get the edits going on *Mechapocalypse*.

15.2

As mentioned, no writing work this past week so nothing new to report. However, I did decide on my plan for getting *Mechapocalypse* to publication. Basically, I'm going to do the edits and then while the book is at my editor's, I'm going to contact a guy through Deviant Art who has some awesome mech images I'd really like to use for a cover. I also decided that I'm going to hire out the lettering for the front cover this time. I usually do this step myself, but I need metallic lettering and that's something outside of my skillset. So I have a guy in mind for that as well.

When all is said and done—and if it all goes to plan—*Mechapocalypse* is going to have a killer cover. I hope it's going to be a killer book, too, but I'll leave that up to you guys to decide.

15.3

Saw *Captain America: The Winter Soldier* this week. Yeah, I know, I'm late to the party. But still . . . glad I saw it. A good movie. Very different from the first one, in my opinion, as this one was more of an espionage flick than a soldier/superhero one. Not that Captain America is your standard superhero, at least, in the movie version. He doesn't duck away into phone booths to transform to go save a damsel in distress. Instead he's a soldier, a soldier who's supposed to be the symbol of an ideal American, maybe even the ideal human. Even as a Canadian I appreciate this because the values Captain America puts forth are transcendent and not limited to a single country. He's very Superman-ish that way.

The twists and turns in the story kept me interested the whole time and for those on this list who know how it ends, I can't help but wonder how they're going to move on from it in *Avengers: Age of Ultron.*

Solid flick.

Like I mentioned last newsletter, I write superhero movie reviews. Made a book called *Look, Up on the Screen! The Big Book of Superhero Movie Reviews.* 100 flicks are covered. It's available here: http://amzn.to/1jVxY31

15.4

As I thought about this week's publishing tip, I thought about how creativity can be applied to marketing your book. As all fine and good as it is to research and look up tricks and techniques for book marketing, I tend to have a real problem with the idea of authors trapping themselves into a kind of marketing "box," that is, only doing what they read and/or are told.

It seems this trap has already ensnared several authors on the Amazon front, in that Amazon tends to be the be all and end all for many. Which is sad, because if you took Amazon out of their marketing/distribution plan, what are they left with? Pretty much nothing. Which is why I preach diversification in terms of one's publication and marketing platform.

Anyway, I can go on and on about the above, but that's not the point here.

Here's the point: when it comes to marketing your books, be creative. Try new things. Take new avenues even if you're the only one doing so.

Some examples:

Say your book centers are apples in some way (i.e. if you wrote *Snow White*) . . . why not give away an apple with every purchase at a book signing or convention appearance?

Why not dress up as the protagonist of your book as a draw to your table?

What if your main character had a pen fetish? Why not give away a pen with each book, one that had your name, the book's title and your website on it?

How about signing bookmarks on top of signing a book? I've signed posters for Axiom-man as well as the books themselves.

Pose for pictures with readers. I've done that. It's fun.

Or for on-line stuff, why not do a temporary promo where someone emails you proof they purchased your book and you send them a short story as a thank you?

These are just ideas off the top of my head. I'm sure with some brainstorming you could come up with a whole bunch more. The idea here is to be creative with your marketing and not just get stuck only doing what you read about. After all, creativity is the business we're in, right? And that extends beyond writing the book itself.

Okay. That's enough from me. Enjoy your week.

Did you know I also write under a pen name?

Two people. One weekend. Love. Sometimes people get to you, underneath, where it counts, in APRIL by Peter Fox
http://amzn.to/cObrh7

End transmission.

Issue Sixteen - August 23, 2014

Hear ye, hear ye.

Welcome to Issue Sixteen of *The Canister X Transmission.*

Sit, and read forth.

16.1

Been in a phase of asking myself why I even bother writing. When I started, it was because I needed a creative outlet. It helped me work through some things. Then when I started looking at making it a career, the financial reward from writing—and some level of fame—became a motivation. Then, later, when I was making money writing and publishing, I wrote because I was having fun doing what I love for a living. And, now, since my meltdown, I'm just writing as something to do. I refuse to let dollars and cents be my reason for it. To me, that's incredibly shallow and a motivation built on shifting sand at best. There needs to be more to a writer's career than just the money side of it. Same with the fame side.

These days, I don't care about the money or the fame. Just writing because it's an area of interest, something to do.

To me, that seems a very pure reason to do it. That means the writing isn't tainted by anything else and is only done for itself.

Of course, this begs the question: well, if you're writing "just because," then why publish or why charge people for your work?

The only answer I have for that is a man's got to eat and feed his family. I'm just glad money isn't a prime—or even secondary—motivator in my career anymore.

There's freedom in that. The search/pursuit of wealth is a prison.

16.2

Editing's underway on *Mechapocalypse.* So far so good. The beginnings of my books are always a bit shaky come second draft because you can see I'm trying to find my footing in the story. The good news is I can revise it so it blends in with the rest of the story when I hit my stride.

Enjoying reading it, and it's reading better than I thought it would, which is a good thing. If I like it, that means there's at least one other person out there who'll like it, too, thus making the whole venture worth it.

16.3

Was at the comic shop yesterday. They have eight to ten Superman toys I want. Each one is twenty to twenty-five bucks. Hoping for one of them for my birthday or Christmas or something. Maybe if I come across some extra cash I'll treat myself and pick one up.

I collect Superman toys of Superman in his original costume, but from different toy series. Didn't realize exactly how many series of toys with him there were out there. This is stuff you don't see on the toy shelves at stores as they are for the collector's market versus mass distribution.

I had a Youtube video of my collection that got deleted in my shut down phase. Been thinking of making a new one showcasing the different Superman toys I got. Just got to find the time to do it.

16.4

Was thinking a bit on how a writer or artist should act in public. Whether that public is on-line or off-, every writer/artist needs to ask themselves what kind of persona they're going to put forth: are they going to play it honest or put on some kind of character.

Some writers play the character of a writer always teetering on the edge of burnout, always busy and talk with an edge. Others are cynical of things, whereas others are super nice and play "the good guy." Some play it very professional and only talk about the craft, never giving their opinion on life events. Others are honest as all get out and give a piece of their mind regardless of consequence.

And other writers are simply themselves, or some combination of the above.

There's really no set piece of advice as to what you should do because arguments can be made for being a character of some sort, and for being yourself.

A character can be a draw and a way to single yourself out amongst the mass of artists and writers out there. If you're known for a certain demeanor, you won't just be another face in the crowd.

At the same time, being yourself can also be a plus because there's an authenticity that comes with just being you. People are drawn to real, down-to-earth, non-pretentious people as well as to "fantasy" figures.

Perhaps the secret is finding out who you really are in this game. This is something that only comes with experience. As has been my own, I've tried character mode in terms of being the creepy horror writer. I've tried the disgruntled journalist approach. Now I'm just being me, warts and all. I've always appreciated people like John Porcellino or Harvey Pekar, those who told it like it is from their point of view with their point of view rooted in their own lives and experiences.

To me, in a world of phonies, there's something special about just being yourself for good or ill. One could even say being yourself in a world full of false fronts can make you a character on your own.

What do you think? What side do you play for? Are you you? Or are you trying to be something/someone else?

Is it working?

Is it real?

Just some thoughts for this week. This is one of those "find out for yourself" marketing tips. There's no real right or wrong answer, but perhaps the only true answer is the one rooted in one's own conviction.

Anyway . . .

Also written under my pen name of Peter Fox:

Sometimes a piece of Heaven comes down to you. Jack finds this out with Cyan in MY ANGEL AND ME http://amzn.to/hkuZkL

End transmission.

Issue Seventeen - August 30, 2014

Once upon a time there was this newsletter called *The Canister X Transmission.*

And now you're reading it.

17.1

This week I'm thankful for the friends I've made in this business. You see, there are two types of people you'll connect with in publishing: those whom you'll simply network with to [hopefully] help each other out, and the other are the genuine friends you'll make. And while you can help each other out career-wise, too, the more important thing you'll take away from it is the deep connection you'll end up sharing.

There are a bunch of guys I've made friends with over the years in this business, the ones who—although we've worked together—are the ones who have stuck with me through thick and thin.

Talked to a guy last weekend—I think it was—and not only have we worked together, but we also share a friendship and were able to talk over some things pertaining to the personal side of this business. Things like goals, personal feelings on the trials and triumphs of publishing, theories on where we think the business is headed, the delicate balance between life and work, being open about how we're feeling these days—things of that nature. The real life stuff.

I'm deeply grateful for those in publishing whom I count as friends. I know that I can talk openly with them and express myself honestly without fear of judgement. I know I can go to them with ideas—or vice versa—and get an honest response as to whether they makes sense or not, or even, simply, if it's a good idea or not.

Behind the words and art on the page, we're all human. To share that humanity with fellow creators is a special thing. It's something I can't do with my "regular" friends and family. I can only do it with those who understand what it's like to have been in the trenches, who've had victories, who've had defeats, and who know what it's like to keep trying even with the odds stacked against you.

These are the relationships that change us. I urge you that if you haven't yet found someone to connect with in this business in that way, to keep an ear to the ground and see who's available and who's willing to not just be a colleague, but a friend as well.

It'll greatly enrich your career and life.

Big time.

17.2

On the work front, this week I resold a short story that I previously sold to another anthology years ago. I consider that a win and the beauty of it is that, aside from edits by this new anthology's editor, the work on it is done. It's nice when you can reuse a story. So that's another publishing credit for me. It was a paying gig, too, which is always nice.

17.3

Saw *X-Men: Days of Future Past.* Extremely well done. I went into it knowing the general gist of the story, but not really knowing what to expect. What I can say is it's a unique X-Men movie compared to the others. Totally different, and it was amazing to see—especially given the time travel element—how the storyline in *Days of Future Past* tied in with the other entries in the saga. They also did well considering that, really, the cast was pretty small compared to the other flicks. That aspect, of course, was part of the story.

Recommended, though they could've done without the few cuss words in it. No real need to include them.

Looking forward to *X-Men: Apocalypse* in 2016.

17.4

There's so much to do in the on-line world when it comes to book/comic marketing. It seems there are a ton of ways to get the word out about your book, social media being the leader of the pack. The problem with social media is there are several social media outlets. It'd be one thing if there were just a couple, but there are tons, with some being more popular than others. The big two are Facebook and Twitter.

The tip for this week is to not use any social media outlet simply as a broadcast point for your work. As much as it would be awesome if they could be, the thing about social media is that it has to be "social" and not just a place for you to spam links about your work.

I'm not saying don't post links. By all means, please do. However, don't let that be all you post. People are naturally resistant to cold sales pitches. Instead, engage your audience with questions, quotes, thoughts of interest, a few life tidbits, and please take the time to reply to others' tweets or Facebook posts.

When it comes to Facebook groups, participate in them. It only takes a few minutes a day to find a few items of interest and comment on them. This shows that you're not just there to sell books. People like networking and authors who aren't just trying to drive sales with "buy my book" links. Building relationships via these platforms is a must for any creator looking to get their name and work out there.

Like I said, however, there are many social media outlets. It is a bit of a job to keep up with however many you're connected with, but if you're able to automate some items and schedule your time accordingly, you'll do just fine. No need to spend the whole day on them.

Moving on, did you know you can read back issues of this newsletter at http://www.tinyletter.com/apfuchs? That's also the same link you can pass onto others who you think would enjoy reading it.

On a side note: I'm a sucker for the supernatural, namely the supernatural from the Judeo/Christian worldview. I wrote a novelette once.

Here's the info:

Painfully tortured for his faith, God opens Duncan's eyes to the spirits responsible. UNDENIABLE http://amzn.to/1cowXfs
End transmission.

Issue Eighteen - September 6, 2014

Welcome to *The Canister X Transmission*, where we tell it like it is. No glamor. No hype.

Just humans creating stuff.

18.1

As I write this I've just finished more or less packing for the Winnipeg Comic and Toy Expo tomorrow. This will be my sixth appearance this year. It's a one-day show from 10 until 5 at the Viscount Gort Hotel here in Winnipeg. Come on by and say hi, if you can. I'll be there tabling, my *Axiom-man* series being the focus. Books'll be just $5 each. Super cheap. I want to spread the word about the series and one of the ways to do that is to put the books on sale. Besides, cons are always a great place for deals.

Also just got off the horn with my editor. Needed to check in with him regarding him doing the edits for *Mechapocalypse.* Nothing like a long distance call down to Florida to discuss business and how much his weather is better than mine. We also touched on a few personal items, too. I've known him since I started publishing back in 2003 and not only are we friends, but we work extremely well together. He's also the kind of guy who doesn't let our friendship get in the way of telling me if my story sucks or not. He's always objective and doesn't give a hoot about my feelings when it comes to work stuff. Couldn't ask for a better editor.

Hoping to also get some editing work done on *Mechapocalypse* today because after talking with my editor, he needs the book ASAP so he can get the edits done in time for me to piece things together for comic con on October 31.

18.2

As mentioned, the plan today is to try and get work done on the second draft of *Mechapocalypse.* I admit I've been slacking in this department and need to pick up the pace if I'm going to make deadline. Now it's crunch time and there's no more room for excuses.

No time to work on it? Find the time.

Tired? Too bad.

Not inspired? Tough beans.

Get. The. Work. Done.

18.3

On the fanboy front, rumors surfaced there's a Supergirl TV series in the works. Nothing in stone, but a pilot's being developed. As a Superman fan, I'm excited. To be honest, I don't know much about Supergirl other than what's been shown on TV before—cartoon and live action—or on the movie screen from that film in the '80s.

A lot of people just want the '80s flick remade because, they say, it was so bad. Personally, I liked that movie despite it being kind of bizarre. It carried with it that Superman tone from the Christopher Reeve films while also trying to do something unique. Or perhaps that's just my childhood talking.

Regardless, I'm interested in seeing what's developed and if this possible new series makes it to air.

18.4

This week I'm going to steal a publishing tip from friend and colleague, graphic novelist GMB Chomichuk.

He and I attended the C4 Lit Fest earlier this year and he said something that's stuck with me, especially since I'm such a hardcore do-it-yourselfer.

He basically said, "Use your strengths. Hire out your weaknesses," when it came to publishing.

We're all good at some things and we all lack in certain areas. This is also true in book production, whether you're doing a novel or graphic novel.

For a lot of novelists, they got the writing part covered, but turning that manuscript into a finished book is where the trick is.

There are writers like me who do pretty much everything from start to finish, then there are others who write the book but hire out formatting, cover design and all the rest. And, hey, I still hire out cover art because I know I can't produce it on my own.

GMB is right. If you don't know how to do something or are weak in a certain area(s), no sense in trying to do it yourself unless you're willing to put in the time to learn how to do it right and/or cultivate the skill to do so. This is why you sometimes see books with terrible covers. The writer didn't hire out his/her weakness and instead tried to do things on their own. Same with improperly formatted books. All the writer thought ahead to was getting the book out there instead of the necessary steps along the way to a quality product and if he or she could handle it.

So I side with GMB Chomichuk in his advice.

Use your strengths. Hire out your weaknesses.

If you're adamant about doing everything yourself, then may I suggest my how-to, step-by-step self-publishing guide, GETTING DOWN AND DIGITAL: HOW TO SELF-PUBLISH YOUR BOOK. It's available on Amazon here: http://amzn.to/1eBljN5

End transmission.

Issue Nineteen - September 13, 2014

Nineteen issues.

An awesome journey.

Welcome.

Read back issues at http://www.tinyletter.com/apfuchs

19.1

For a long time I was merciless when it came to getting the writing work done. So much so I preached a message of basically, "It doesn't matter what's going on in your life, if you want to make it in this field, you shut up and do the work."

Not anymore.

See, lately real life has been getting in the way of me getting done all that I want to. You got a 9-5, a family, household responsibilities—it's hard to squeeze in the extra time to write. It takes discipline to do that because essentially being a writer "on the side" is like having a second job. The only difference is it's a job you work from home and have some flexibility on because you have no one breathing down your neck to go-go-go. Therefore, it's easy to not do it.

I used to tell people that the writing work comes first, everything else second. And while there's truth to my message of "If you want to make it, you got to put the time in," I've come to realize that, yes, indeed other things happen that get in the way of achieving the dream. It sucks, but it's reality.

I guess what I'm saying is I have more grace now for things getting in the way of getting the work done. Laziness isn't an excuse nor is procrastination, but things like getting the house ready for winter or spending time with your kids because they haven't seen you all week are real reasons to skip the writing session.

In the end, I'm coming around to the idea that it's all about balance while keeping in mind that what you put into something is usually what you get out of it. The whole "reap what you sow" thing.

Simply put: get the work done, but don't sacrifice the things that are truly important like family.

19.2

In work news, I finished Draft Two of *Mechapocalypse* and have typed up the edits for it. A fresh manuscript has been printed out for Draft Three and I plan on starting that after a short break after sending out this newsletter. So that's the plan for today. I'd like to get about a third of the Draft Three edits done before the day is out. If I do another third tomorrow then the final third Monday, I can type up the edits Tuesday and email the file to my editor right after. After that, I'll give him the week or two he needs to go over it before I get it back to go through his suggestions and changes. Once that's done, I'll edit it once more myself then it's off to my wife as a first time reader. Then the book is yours, nicely packaged between two mech-covered covers.

19.3

The other day Zack Snyder released a revealing photo of the new batmobile for *Batman v Superman: Dawn of Justice.* While we kind of saw it behind Ben Affleck's Batman in the batsuit reveal pic, now we get to see it in all its glory. It's like a cross between the '89 Keaton batmobile and the tumbler from the Christopher Nolan films. What's strange is it has a machine gun mounted in the middle. I don't expect Batman to use lethal force because that's not his thing, so perhaps he'll use it as an intimidation item or blast open doors with it or something like he did in the '89 movie.

Time will tell.

Regardless, it looks like an incredible machine and, while I haven't seen it in action aside from a leaked video of it driving behind a camera truck, it appears this batmobile will be the sickest one yet to grace the silver screen.

19.4

This week's publishing/marketing tip is also a life tip, one I've learned since my meltdown.

Take things one thing at a time.

While this is directed toward the first- or second-time author, there's a lesson in it for all of us.

Publishing can be daunting, especially if it's your first rodeo, with all sorts of things to do and keep in mind. You do your research and you hear everything about minding your formatting, to legalities with your cover artist, to setting up your Facebook and Twitter, to marketing your website, to setting up signings, to working with an editor, to possibly using beta readers and . . . yikes! It can all quickly become overwhelming.

It's my opinion for life and for publishing to slow down and do each task one at a time, without giving thought to the rest of the things on your to-do list.

It's like those of us who lay awake at night because our head is racing with our checklists. It's a waste of time and energy because, frankly, you're lying in bed, it's late and there's nothing you can do about those things at that moment anyway. Why think about them?

Same with publishing/marketing.

When sitting down to complete whatever task, just simply focus on the task at hand, pushing out of your mind the rest of the things on your list. If you need to, make a list—in order, if possible—of all the things you need to do. Get them out of your head and onto paper. After that, don't think about the items except for that first one. Why waste mental energy thinking about other things instead of focusing that same energy to do the best you can on the task in front of you? Why divide yourself? Then, once that first task is done, cross it off and move onto the next one. It'll make this publishing ride so much smoother.

I'm speaking from experience. I used to multi-task like crazy and while there's a time and place to do two or three things at once, it makes more sense to focus yourself on one thing instead of getting stressed about items further down the list.

Working at full potential on each item will yield better results.

It goes this way for life, too. Take things one thing at a time instead of letting your head go into a tailspin about everything that needs to be done.

Simplify.

It's simply the best choice.

Okay, that's it for this week.

If you like these behind-the-scenes/down-to-earth ideas and need more inspiration for your writing and publishing, consider my book CANADIAN SCRIBBLER: COLLECTED LETTERS OF AN UNDERGROUND WRITER. They'll give you a boost! http://amzn.to/1eYrNLn

End transmission.

Issue Twenty - September 20, 2014

The twentieth issue on the twentieth of the month. How 'bout that?

Welcome to *The Canister X Transmission.*

20.1

Smoking.

A disgusting habit, when you get right down to it: inhaling toxic chemicals into your lungs. Yet, it's oh so enjoyable.

I started when I was eighteen, having smoked on and off before then. Smoked all the way up until November of 2012 then quit cold turkey. Was clean for sixteen months, but in April of this year I got it into my head to start again and, after a month of fighting the urge, finally caved in May. Now I'm a smoker again and, while enjoyable, I know I got to quit. It's bad for you, it's expensive, it's not healthy for the people around you and, really, it's just plain dumb.

But, again, enjoyable.

Yesterday a friend gave me a vape pen, which is basically an electronic cigarette, kind of the size of a cigar. You load the nicotine and various flavors into it and "smoke" that instead of burning a cigarette. It's battery operated and gives you a sensation similar to smoking while also delivering nicotine into your system. The difference is there are no other chemicals. Just the flavoring—of which there are a plethora of kinds—and the nicotine itself. In fact, I'm puffing on it as I write this newsletter.

You can control the nicotine levels, anywhere from very high to minimal to, I think, none at all. The idea is to either use the vape pen as a "cleaner" substitute for smoking or as a quitting device. I'm using it for the latter because eventually I want to stop altogether. This is a good bridge between cigarettes and, well, smoking nothing.

Anyone on this list use a vape pen? What do you think about it?

Apparently I'll start to feel better using it, too, as I'm not getting all the other crud that's in cigarettes into my system so my body will have more energy instead of spending that energy fighting off the garbage.

It does take some getting used to because it's not 100% interchangeable with a cigarette. It does help take the edge off of cravings though.

Time will tell, but so far I'm enjoying it.

20.2

Last night I sent off Draft Three of *Mechapocalypse* to my editor. Looking forward to seeing his thoughts and I hope the edits I receive back aren't horrendous. I wrote a fairly clean book error-wise. There wasn't a lot of redrafting. Just tweaks and fixes, a few spelling issues and a bit of grammar. Story-wise everything was fine except for a couple continuity issues, which I corrected.

Yeah, should be okay.

Also got in touch with the cover guy and we're ironing out the final details so he can get to work creating an exciting cover for it.

So far we're on track to make deadline for the Central Canada Comic Con at the end of October.

20.3

In fanboy news, they've green lit a Deadpool movie due out in 2016. It's been in development for ages, but now is finally going forward. I'm excited. Not that I'm a huge Deadpool fan, but I saw the test footage that was leaked onto the Net and it looked crazy good, the scene about Deadpool in a car with a bunch of goons and he takes them out.

He's also a funny character yet utterly serious in terms of what he does.

Deadpool's insanely popular at comic shows, with all sorts of folks dressed up as him. He's got a video game, was in *X-Men Origins: Wolverine*, and a bunch of T-shirts, hats, etc.

It was only a matter of time before he got a feature flick.

Personally, I think that test footage was "leaked" on purpose to gauge fan reaction because not long after it came out, it was announced they were making a movie.

Hmmm . . .

20.4

If there's one thing that sells a book, it's reviews. The more positive reviews for a title, the more it's going to sell. People are "bandwagon" kind of creatures like that.

(Oddly, I've also seen it where a book has tons of bad reviews and it was still selling like hotcakes. Perhaps people were buying it to see what all the negative fuss was about?)

The problem with reviews is you need them to sell a lot of books, but need to sell a lot of books to get them.

A Catch 22.

While the art of getting reviews is too big a topic for the space allotted in this newsletter, I will offer a tip to help you get them.

Consider offering the book for free—whether in print or electronic edition—to six to twelve people whom you think will enjoy it. They can be friends, family, fellow writers, etc. Tell them flat out that you're offering them the book for free in exchange for a review.

An *honest* review.

While, of course, you hope it'll be positive, don't be the author who gives the book away in exchange for positive feedback only. What I mean is, don't make that a condition of the giveaway. Instead, simply offer it for review and ask them to have it done by such-and-such a date and for them to post their review, at minimum, on Amazon. If they can post the same review on other retailer sites when the book is available, that's great, too.

By giving this book away, you're obviously forfeiting that half dozen to a dozen possible sales, but at the same time, you could be gaining many more sales back thanks to the reviews they leave.

Fair trade.

If you want to see a fair mix of good and not-so-good reviews, here's a link to one of my own titles and a little commercial:

First came the rain. Then came the screams. Then came the undead. BLOOD OF THE DEAD, a time travel zombie novel. http://amzn.to/18p4VSt

End transmission.

Issue Twenty-one - September 27, 2014

Welcome to the Issue Twenty-one of *The Canister X Transmission.*

This issue would be a boon for black jack.

Get it? Get it?

Ah, never mind.

21.1

Too many projects.

And I blame Warren Ellis.

See, he's got my head spinning again. I get his *Orbital Operations* newsletter and in the last one he started talking about thinking about doing a long black and white graphic novel. Then, to make things worse, he invoked Dave Sim, who's a comics creator I greatly admire and have had correspondence with over the years (see my *Canadian Scribbler: Collected Letters of an Underground Writer*). So now he's got me thinking—yet again—about doing a long black and white graphic novel(s).

I love black and white comics. Give me those over color books any day. To me, it takes a great artist to work without—or not rely on—color to make the artwork stand on its own. I find today's color comics too busy with flashy color tricks and gradients and airbrushing and all that nonsense. Even for color comics, I prefer the straight, single-tone ones, you know, where green was green and not Robin's pant leg being a strange mix of emerald and jade.

But that's just me.

So yeah, thanks a lot, Warren Ellis. Now you got my head busy when I've got, well, let's see, five and a half novels to write, a graphic novel to finish, plus a bunch of other stuff that's part idea/part notes to take care of.

Never mind the business end of all this.

Of course, I realize I'm not the only writer who struggles with too many ideas. The problem is simply an issue of maintaining continuous mental energy and time to write them all down.

There's only one solution and it's a simple one: tackle them one at a time. You put one foot in front of the other, eventually you'll get where you're going.

So, again, thanks a lot, Warren Ellis.

You're keeping me inspired.

21.2

Work update: got the edits back from that short story I sold to that anthology. Went over them. Accepted most of them. Some were just a matter of taste. The next step in the process is to read the story one final time myself to catch anything else, then that's it. It gets handed in and the draft I hand in will pretty much be what's read in the book save for, maybe, one or two minor edits done on the publisher's end before press. (i.e. dumb stuff we didn't catch like "there" and "their," things like that.)

Also got *Mechapocalypse* back from my editor the other day. I haven't looked at it yet. Been wanting to, but given my philosophy of doing things one thing at a time, I have to get this short story draft out of the way before I can go over my editor's edits on the book. I don't expect them to be drastic.

Also got the final cover art in for *Mechapocalypse*. It's killer. A very fresh kind of cover compared to what's been on my other books. The only changes that need to be made are me adding the plot synopsis on the back and possibly bumping the front cover text around to fit the printer's template properly. No biggie.

On track for a late October release.

21.3

Arrow Season Two came out not long ago. It's on my to-buy list. I loved the first season and I've heard nothing but good things about the second one.

See, I don't have cable and I'm not one to normally stream things off the Internet without paying for it, so I've been waiting until Season Two hit Dvd so I can binge watch the entire thing.

Season Three starts up soon and, like I mentioned a few newsletter back, I'm thinking of getting cable to watch it.

Season Two first, though.

21.4

You get a marketing tip this week.

Author interviews.

Consider hosting some on your website. Not only are they a good way to connect with other writers—regardless of where they fall on the "famous" list—but they also give insight into what makes the other guy tick. Further, they can be a traffic booster to your site, thus drawing attention to what you do. The idea here is the author you interview has fans. You do an interview with them, you advertise it, so do they, and their fans come to your site to check out the interview, in turn putting the spotlight on you as well.

Make sense?

You can conduct the interview several ways. One is to engage in an email dialogue with them and print that. Another is to do the same, but also break that dialogue up into a Q & A. Yet another way is to send them a list of personalized questions and ask them to fill it out and get it back to you. The final way is for you to have a standard set of questions for every writer you interview. You send the questions to them, they fill it out, and you run that.

If you have any other ideas on how to do this, reply to this newsletter and let me know. I'm all ears.

Speaking of ears, listen to this:

Angels. Demons. Giant zombies. A war is raging. POSSESSION OF THE DEAD, a time travel zombie thriller. http://amzn.to/1fvlf7g

End transmission.

Issue Twenty-two - October 4, 2014

Issue Twenty-two. I'm seeing double.

Welcome.

22.1

Celebrating the victories.

It's an overlooked step in the creative process and, perhaps, the longer someone has been doing something creative, the more apt the person is to *not* celebrate the victories along the way.

Case in point, soon I'll have *Mechapocalypse* off to press. The book will be done. Done-done. Since I don't recall celebrating completing the book's first draft in May, I plan on rewarding myself for a job well done once the book is at the printer. Whether this means treating myself to a McMeal or taking some time off, I don't know. Might even go to the movies. Regardless, I need to take a moment and be proud of myself for putting another book to bed. I've written and published thirty of them or so. At this point, to be honest, it's no big deal to me.

But it should be.

Finishing a creative project, going straight through from idea to completion, is something any artist should be proud of no matter how many times they've done it. Taking a moment and stepping back and saying, "Yeah, I made that," is an important step in the creative process. It is affirmation that one can see something through start to finish, that they've done their best in completing it, and that they're proud of what they did. I mean, if you're not proud of your project, why put it out there, right?

That's not to put completing a book or graphic novel or even oneself up on a pedestal. That's not what I'm saying. What I am saying is to take pleasure in a job well done, perhaps as self-encouragement to venture down that road again.

Nothing wrong with being pleased in what you made. Even God was happy after He made the Earth and all that was within it.

Of course, publishing a book is of a way lesser magnitude, but you get the idea.

In the end, it's okay to encourage yourself, be happy with your creation, and look forward to the next one.

I'm looking forward to celebrating.

22.2

Subtle title change announcement: *Mechapocalypse* is now called *Mech Apocalypse.* I've been thinking of making the change for a while and after my cover guy put it as such on the cover he submitted, I decided to make it official. That, and it helps people from mispronouncing it. Likewise, the upcoming sequels will, of course, bear the same change.

As of this writing, I'm going through the book one final time. This is my last kick at the can to make sure the book is error free and is written as best as possible. It's already mostly formatted with all that's left being to add in the headers and footers, some title graphics and any small changes to the actual text.

Almost there.

22.3

Today my kids are watching *Mystery Men*, which is a terribly underrated movie. It's funny, smart, and, between the lines, is an interesting commentary on the superhero genre. Nobody really talks about it these days, but to me it's a gem of a flick that I like popping into the player now and then for a good time.

Highly recommended.

I reviewed it in my book, *Look, Up on the Screen!* You can find out more info about this title here: http://amzn.to/1jVxY31

22.4

Last week I talked about interviewing other authors for your website in the hopes of boosting your web traffic. This week I want to talk about being interviewed yourself.

Interviews are a good way to increase exposure about you and your work. Depending on who's listening/watching/reading the interview, it can also lead to increased sales.

There are two main avenues of interviews: traditional media and the Internet.

For traditional media like TV, radio, the newspaper and magazines, I suggest crafting a press release that you can send out. A press release is basically a brief pitch on you, your book and it gives info on why you should be interviewed. There are lots of examples on-line as to how to craft one and lay one out, which is beyond the scope of this newsletter. A good resource for crafting your release can be found at: http://www.wikihow.com/Write-a-Press-Release

Send this release out to your local media, whether that's the local TV station, newspaper, radio and more. You can usually find info on their websites in terms of who/where to send press releases to.

For Internet sites, there are a number of options. I suggest sending a query letter with your name, book title, a brief synopsis and a short explanation as to why you should be interviewed on their site.

Be genre specific. If you've written a sci-fi, no point in being interviewed on a horror or romance website, you know?

Places to be interviewed at on-line:

- author websites
- book blogs
- on-line magazines (depending on their nature, send a press release instead)
- genre-specific review sites
- on-line radio programs or podcasts (send press release)

- Facebook groups (if they host interviews)

Go to the websites you want to be interviewed at, collect their email, then send out your pitch en mass to save yourself sending out the same email over and over again. Use the Bcc option to blind copy everyone so their emails addresses don't show up in each other's inbox.

Wait and see what happens. Some will reply, some not. Don't harass anyone. If they say no, leave it alone. Thank them for their time and move on. If they say yes, follow their instructions on how they want to do things. And, of course, thank them for their time. Be honest in your answers and write them out as best you can, error free. Mention your book, but don't mention it with every answer as that's too transparent.

Once the interview comes out, advertise it on your site, Twitter, Facebook, etc. to get people to see it.

That's the short version on how to do this.

For examples of interviews, you can see the ones I've done at: http://canisterx.com/interviews/

And now . . .

Zombies. The devil. War. A wild adventure through a post-apocalyptic world. REDEMPTION OF THE DEAD. http://amzn.to/1rFWKWm

End transmission.

Issue Twenty-three - October 11, 2014

This is the twenty-third issue of *The Canister X Transmission.*

Thank you for joining me.

23.1

"But hey, man, every day is a brand new deal, right? Just keep on working and something's bound to turn up." - Harvey Pekar

True words. Sometimes all you got to do is to keep on keeping on.

In a work season myself. I'm going to press on *Mech Apocalypse* tomorrow; have some suddenly-dropped-in-my-lap publishing business work to do after that; need to prep for Comic Con, which is at the end of the month; launch *Mech Apocalypse* hopefully next weekend; finish up my cosplay for the con; and keep up with this newsletter.

I don't know what's going to come of any of it. Though I think of the [hopefully] good times that'll come from the fruit of my labors, I'm trying not to live in the future as per my "take it one thing at a time" motto.

Sometimes all you can do is to keep on working. That head needs to be kept down sometimes lest you get distracted about the other things that need doing. At the same time, little bits of positivity can show up along the way.

For example, I know I'll be selling at least one copy of *Mech Apocalypse* at Comic Con. Had a guy tell me he was really interested in it during the last show I did at the beginning of September.

I look forward to the good feelings that'll pop up inside of me as I check off the different parts of that business work I have to do.

I'm sure my cosplay will help bring people to my table at Comic Con as folks tend to ask for pictures of character costumes they really like. What a good opportunity to show them my books! But I know just completing the costume will give me a boost in self-esteem.

And *Mech Apocalypse*. If I steadily plug away at it tomorrow, it'll be done and off to press. Another book down. That's pressure taken off my shoulders and another door opened to help put food on the table for my family.

Things will turn up when you keep on working. But that's the key: you got to keep on working.

Or, as Robert Crumb put it, "Keep on truckin'."

23.2

As mentioned, I'm going to press on *Mech Apocalypse* tomorrow. Normally, tomorrow is Thanksgiving Sunday here in Canada, but I'm celebrating it today with family and then again on Monday, leaving tomorrow wide open to get the work done and get the book out.

My wife is finishing up reading it as first reader. That'll be done before the day is out, I'm hoping, so that tomorrow all I need to do is type up final edits and finish formatting the book for paperback and eBook. Then it's done and off to the printer and the various eBook distributors. The eBook edition will probably be available as early as Monday, with the print edition to follow later in the week.

Next Saturday I plan on launching the book on-line with the off-line launch to be at Comic Con starting October 31.

23.3

This week I got *Sunnyville Stories* Volume 2 (http://amzn.to/1p1uBHV) in the mail direct from its creator, Max West.

I'm a fan of this graphic novel series. It's about a cat named Rusty who comes to the small town of Sunnyville and ends up getting involved with one adventure after another. What I enjoy about the series is its simplicity, that is, each episode contained in each volume has a beginning, middle and end, and has a point to them, or a moral of some kind. Kind of like the old cartoons from the '80s. Remember those what-did-we-learn-today episode recaps at the end? It feels like that when you read *Sunnyville Stories.*

The artwork is clean and concise and is delivered in glorious black and white.

Each episode is also released as a stand-alone issue, but I've been collecting the trade paperbacks.

It's worth checking out. You can visit *Sunnyville Stori*es on-line at www.sunnyvillestories.com

23.4

The past couple of newsletters I've been talking about author interviews, with the first installment about hosting other authors on your blog/website, the next about yourself being interviewed.

To wrap it up, this week I want to talk about how to conduct yourself during an interview.

See here we go.

There's two kinds you'll be doing: in-person and distant.

For in-person interviews, like for television/Internet streaming and radio/podcasts, you need to be mindful of a couple things.

One, always have a copy of your book on hand for a quick visual plug (i.e. lifting it up when referencing it in the interview).

Two, grooming. You don't have to wear a suit and tie or fancy dress, but it would be good to come across as a professional, so I suggest dressing business casual. Comb your hair, clean up the beard, brush your teeth.

Three, be animated. I'm not talking act like Pee Wee Herman, but use hand gestures, smile, a twinkle in your eyes—a genuine excitement about your book. This kind of behavior comes out in your voice and makes it more engaging for the listener/viewer.

Four, be yourself. Don't put up a phony front or come off as a pretentious writer. Just play it casual. Yes, take it seriously, but don't get worked up over it. You're simply talking to another human being after all, something you do all the time in your day-to-day life anyway. The person interviewing you puts their pants on one leg at a time like you do, too, so don't sweat it. If you stumble in your words, so what? Start over. Just talk to them like you're talking to a friend. Listeners/viewers like folks who are down-to-earth. Pepper a little humor in there. People like jokes. They put not just the listeners/viewers at ease, but you and the interviewer as well.

It really is that easy.

For distant interviews, like ones you'd do over email, it doesn't matter what you wear or what you sound like because no one's going to see you anyway. (Obviously.)

Aside from being yourself as mentioned above, you do need to be careful of one thing: the writing. You *are* a writer, after all. You need to make sure that your answers are free of spelling and grammatical errors because when it comes to these kinds of interviews, there's no editor who's doing to do a "second draft" for you. What you submit is usually what gets printed, so be careful. Read over your replies several times and tweak as necessary. Run a spellcheck if you want to as well.

As a general rule for both kinds of interviews—because this is a promo opportunity we're talking about—it's important to mention your book a few times throughout it. Likewise, you can mention other titles in your backlist. However, don't form every answer around your book, as in, "My book this, my book that." That'll turn the reader/listener/viewer off and you just ruined your chance to sell them on your title. Mention it here and there, otherwise leave it alone.

Usually, there's an opportunity during these interviews to mention a website or your Twitter address or something, so take advantage of that. If people want to know more, they'll look you up.

That about sums up this week's marketing tip and our series on author interviews. Hope you've found them useful.

In other news . . .

What happens when someone gives you superpowers but doesn't say what they're for? Find out in AXIOM-MAN http://amzn.to/1khtYfz

End transmission.

Issue Twenty-four - October 18, 2014

Welcome to *The Canister X Transmission*, brought to you weekly by A.P. Fuchs and Coscom Entertainment.

24.1

With things wrapped up on *Mech Apocalypse*—on-line launch coming soon once the paperback listings update—I have no pressing deadlines. The sequel is half-written and I plan to finish that once I do an in-between project, which is . . .

A graphic novel.

I thought of a concept this week that I really want to explore in comic book form, one that I would write and draw. I wrote up a treatment for it and the next step is to outline it, basically a scene-by-scene thing. After that, I'll take that outline and turn it into a full-fledged comic book script. I suspect the graphic novel will be over a hundred pages long when fully written given the scope of the story.

Interestingly, the concept would also make a good novel and, though I never outline for my novels, once the outline for the project is complete, I'd be at a kind of crossroads, that is, I *could* simply flesh out the outline and make it a book. It's in a popular genre, which in turn might make it a shoe-in for mainstream success. At the same time, I really want to get back to my comic book roots—have been for years—so I'm a little torn at what to do. Should I chase the dollar sign or the art? I've always preached art first, money later. Perhaps this is a test to see if I can also walk-the-walk and not just talk-the-talk?

At the same time, once the script for the comic is done, to do a novel adaptation would be quite easy. Maybe this story will be released in two formats? A graphic novel and a book?

The beauty of the concept stage, where ideas can go in any direction.

But, yeah, comics. An incredible medium and one I really want to get back to. Plus, doing this story as a graphic novel would be a chance for me to stretch my creative muscles because not only is the writing of a comic script different than writing prose, I'd also get to play around and draw. It was drawing, after all, that eventually led me to writing books.

More as this develops.

24.2

Last Sunday I went to press on *Mech Apocalypse*. The paperback files were at the printer all week and today I let the printer know they can go ahead and make physical books out of them (takes time for processing). In the next day or so, the on-line listings for the paperback edition will start to appear. However, the eBook version has been ready since I uploaded it last Sunday and has been available. I've kept things more or less on the down-low because I'm waiting for the paperback listings to manifest before I go ahead and do my on-line marketing blitz. But for you, dear reader, I want to make it known via this newsletter that the eBook for *Mech Apocalypse* is available for download at various eBook sites (i.e. Smashwords, DriveThru Fiction, Kindle) and the Kindle link for the book is here: http://amzn.to/1sIfrMR

Here's the short version of the synopsis:

A Stolen Weapon. A Rising Enemy. A Change to History.

All goes haywire when a secret weapon is activated and an evil thought vanquished returns. Riley and Sophie find themselves in a place different from the world they left yet also familiar.

From high-flying exo-suit battles to giant mech-bots exchanging missile fire, this is an action-packed military sci-fi adventure you won't want to miss!

Thank you in advance for your support.

24.3

This past week was a big week in superhero movie news. On Wednesday Warner Bros. announced their DC Comics superhero movie slate all the way up to 2020.

It's as follows:

Batman v Superman: Dawn of Justice, 2016
Suicide Squad, 2016
Wonder Woman, 2017
Justice League Part One, 2017
The Flash, 2018
Aquaman, 2018
Shazam, 2019
Justice League Part Two, 2019
Cyborg, 2020
Green Lantern, 2020

Not to mention the solo Superman and Batman movies apparently also in the works.

This is huge news for guys like me who are longing for DC Comics to have their day in the sun. The box office is all Marvel right now and, as a DC fan, it's super exciting to see DC/WB finally get their act together and come out with a plan. It sucks that I still have to wait two years to finally see the first movie on the slate, but at least it's coming out.

Personally, I'm looking most forward to *Batman v Superman*, *Justice League* Parts One and Two, and *Wonder Woman*.

Which flicks do you anticipate the most?

24.4

With more and more book shoppers switching to on-line buying, it has its advantages and disadvantages. One of the disadvantages is you're dealing with not actually seeing/handling the product aside from a picture or two. When it comes to books, this makes the cover art all the more important. At the same time, it puts those of us who publish on-line in an unfortunate place because we can't hand the reader a copy of the book to peruse through. However, we can create a similar experience by making it possible for the reader to virtually "flip through" the book via Amazon's Search Inside program. It's free and a valuable asset for creators who rely mostly on on-line sales.

This also applies to comics and graphic novels, too.

How it works is you upload your book's front and back cover files along with its interior to Amazon and what it does is it enables buyers to click on your book's cover and read bits and pieces of the book before buying. They can't read the whole thing despite you uploading the entire interior, but they can read a few pages, just like they would at the bookstore. From what I understand, it also helps with keywords when folks search for books at Amazon because, by uploading your interior, you're providing all sorts of metadata to Amazon's search engine. (i.e. if you have lots of robots in your book and you use the word "robot" a lot, it should help your book's ranking in the search results for those looking for robot stories.) In short, it brings more attention to your book.

The web address to do this is www.sellercentral.amazon.com

As mentioned, you'll need image files of your front and back covers along with the interior of your book. You'll identify these files with the book's ISBN. Make sure your image files are 300 dpi, RGB, JPEG.

i.e.

ISBN-frontcover.jpeg
ISBN-backcover.jpeg
ISBN.pdf

Put these in a zip file of ISBN.zip and upload that.

There, you're done and once the system updates, folks'll be able to search through your book.

Want to reach me elsewhere on the web? I can be found at canisterx.com, facebook.com/apfuchsbooks and twitter.com/ap_fuchs

Newly endowed with superpowers, Gabriel must decide what to do with them. See him as Axiom-man in his FIRST NIGHT OUT at http://amzn.to/1fpeJPv

End transmission.

Issue Twenty-five - October 25, 2014

The twenty-fifth issue of *The Canister X Transmission* on the 25th. Funny how the dates have been lining up lately.

Welcome aboard.

25.1

This week is comic con prep week. Lots to do. I have to get my book stock in order, see how many copies I have of what, set aside X amount of copies of each title, and pack them up. I also need to get my signage together, promo items, float, and cosplay together. Let's not forget the all-important display. I might have mentioned it before but this year I'm downsizing to just one table instead of my usual three. The plan is to display everything vertically instead of horizontally. I think this will make for a more attractive display and convey me more as a "big deal" since people tend to be impressed by/drawn to larger displays. A bit of psychological marketing, if you will.

Copies of the new *Mech Apocalypse* and extra copies of *Axiom-man* shipped the other day. Here's hoping they get here on time as I'd really like to showcase the new book and I'm down to my last handful of copies of *Axiom-man.* I plan on putting the series on special next weekend so need to have books on hand to meet demand.

Also coming together is my cosplay for the show. I plan on wearing my Batman onesie on the Friday—which is the classic blue and gray batsuit—and my main cosplay on Saturday and Sunday. We have all the items we need for this year's cosplay but the Mrs. needs to sew parts together, cut up others and make the whole thing work. Thank goodness I have a wife who knows how to do costumes.

Other than all the above, I'm ready for the show, which pretty much means I'm excited and mentally ready. It's all the extraneous stuff I need to get together so I'm ready-ready. I hope to have stuff finalized before the day is out on most of it, however.

25.2

I came up with a graphic novel concept the other week so wrote out a treatment for it. After that was done, I wrote out a scene-by-scene outline. Now I need to take those scenes and flesh them out. The good part is the creative heavy lifting is done in terms of what happens. To take that and simply expand on it for a panel-by-panel presentation should be pretty straight forward.

I've tried different comic scripting methods over the years. I used to write full script, then I've done the Harvey Pekar method of writing the story via panels and stick figures. Now I'm trying this method of blocking out the story first then filling in the gaps later. So far, I like this last method. Really breaks down the process and makes the whole thing feel easier.

We'll see how the rest of it goes.

25.3

This week Marvel unleashed the *Avengers: Age of Ultron* trailer on the world. It was fantastic! You got to see the team in action again along with a cool voiceover and soundtrack. Further, you got to see the Hulkbuster Iron Man armor. No idea how that's going to play into the thing, but it's definitely got me interested.

In terms of the story, nothing was revealed except the villain, Ultron. For what the flick will be about specifically, I guess we'll have to wait for another trailer for that.

Still, May can't get here soon enough. I'm excited to see the follow-up to one of the highest-grossing films of all time. Not that that's a draw for me. I don't care how much money it made, but obviously Marvel did something the right the first time around otherwise the film wouldn't have done as good as it had.

25.4

One thing you can do when marketing your book is "max out" one of the other things you use: e-mail. Why not mention your book in your email's signature line? You send out X amount of e-mails every day, after all, so might as well let whoever you're sending them to know about your book.

Keep it brief, exciting, then post a link to where your book can be purchased at the end.

I re-use my book tweets for my e-mail signature line.

Some examples:

First came the rain. Then came the screams. Then came the undead. BLOOD OF THE DEAD, a time travel zombie novel. http://amzn.to/18p4VSt

Angels. Demons. Giant zombies. A war is raging. POSSESSION OF THE DEAD, a time travel zombie thriller. http://amzn.to/1fvlf7g

Zombies. The devil. War. A wild adventure through a post-apocalyptic world. REDEMPTION OF THE DEAD. http://amzn.to/1rFWKWm

You can also put them on rotation and change your e-mail signature line, say, once every couple weeks or once a month or something, to keep marketing your other titles should you have them.

The more ways you can talk about your book on-line, the better.

Speaking of signature lines:

High-flying exo-suit battles & giant mech-bots exchange missile fire in the military sci-fi novel MECH APOCALYPSE! http://amzn.to/1sIfrMR

End transmission.

Issue Twenty-six - October 31, 2014

Welcome to *The Canister X Transmission.* You're getting this issue a day early because I'm at Winnipeg's C4 Comic Con this weekend and won't be able to send it out Saturday.

It's Tuesday as I write this.

26.1

Been ruminating a bit on my career, really taking a look at where I'm at. I've come a long way since I started writing in 2000. I've published over 30 books, a bunch of comics, been published in anthologies and magazines, etc. I've published over 100 books for other people and met a bunch of great people—famous and non- —along the way. (See www.canisterx.com/bibliography for my complete bibliography.) These days, with my company shut down in terms of publishing others, I'm kind of back to square one again where it's just me and my stuff. And I don't really have a whole lot to show for it, at least in terms of being a commercially successful writer. I suppose a lot of it is my own doing. I did write "fringe" fiction after all—independent superhero stuff—and poured my energies into other people's careers instead of my own. I don't regret my decisions, by any means, but now with this big publishing boom, a flooded market, and so many writers out there, I feel like I've missed my chance.

This is where you say: No, no, you keep trying, keep pushing.

And I agree with you because I'm stubborn as a mule and once I put my mind to accomplishing something, you can consider that thing as good as done.

I guess what I'm saying is not only do I feel like a bit of a failure, I also am indifferent toward it. The reason being is there's a sense of accomplishment I can't shake. I only know of one other writer who's walked a similar path to me. Everyone else I know in the biz hasn't done what I've done. Not tooting my own horn, just saying what's on the inside. At the end of the day, I'm at a place where should my career end here and now, I'd be fine with it. I've done a lot. I've given a lot. I've sacrificed more than most people know to try and make this writing thing happen.

That's got to count for something.

No, I don't have any plans to retire anytime soon. I think what's happening is I've achieved a level of success that only comes after years of dedicated effort. The success I'm talking about is that sense of completion of doing what you set out to do, the ability to look at one's own career and be fine with just writing stories regardless of how many readers actually read it.

The ability to take pride in one's own work and for that pride to be payment enough for a job well done.

Yeah, that counts for something.

Maybe I'm not a failure after all.

26.2

In the interest of writing out my upcoming projects, here's a list of works to be completed. The plan is to publish them as I finish them and I hope to knock off the following in the next three years.

Titles and dates presented where applicable.

Fox (graphic novel: outlined) - 2015

Mech Apocalypse 2 (1/2 completed) - 2015

Robot City (3/4 completed) - 2015

Mech Apocalypse 3

Axiom-man Episode No. 3: Rumblings (Prequel to the *Battle of Power Trilogy*) - 2015

Axiom-man Book 5 (*Battle of Power Trilogy* Part One)

The Canister X Transmission: Year One (in progress) - 2015

Axiom-man Episode No. 4 (*Battle of Power Trilogy* Part Two)

Canadian Scribbler: Collected Letters of an Underground Writer Vol. 2 (in progress)

Getting Down and Digital: How to Market Your Book

The Girl That Got Away (writing as Peter Fox; completed) – 2015

Axiom-man Book 6 (*Battle of Power Trilogy* Part Three)

Meet the Maximums (graphic novel; prequel story complete)

Axiom-man: Tenth Anniversary Special Edition – 2016

Axiom-man: The Cobalt Crusader (short story collection; 3 tales written) – 2016

The order of the above might get switched around, depending on what the muse dictates, but those projects should be enough to keep me plenty busy over the next few years. I have ideas for a couple more things, but the list as shown is priority for now.

26.3

Things are coming together for my cosplay for the Central Canada Comic Con this weekend. What am I going as?

Spider-Man Noir.

Got almost everything together and the bulk of the sewing done.

I love this costume! It's an incredibly unique take on the Spidersuit. (For those who don't know, *Spider-Man Noir* was a miniseries published by Marvel some years back. This version of Spider-Man also appeared in the videogame, *Spider-Man: Shattered Dimensions.*)

I'll be suited up Saturday and Sunday at the show. Come by my table and we'll take a picture together or something.

26.4

Fliers.

They're valuable tools to market your books. They're easy to make, cheap to print. They're ideal for book signings and conventions.

Make a flier about your book(s). Something simple. Put your cover on it, its ISBN info, a brief 2-3-sentence synopsis, where it's available, your website, a splashy headline at the top and away you go.

It's like a business card, only bigger. You can fit four onto a standard 8.5 x 11" piece of paper. Lay them out on the computer, print them out at home. Black and white is fine, so is color.

The idea here is to provide a simple sheet of paper with direct info about your book. Like I said, you can put more than one book on it. Divide the quarter sheet in half, with a book cover on each side. Need more room? Use half an 8.5 x 11", whether lengthwise or widthwise. There really are no rules. You just want to provide a "go to" piece of information about your book(s).

I don't know why authors don't use these. They can be left at the freebie table at conventions, on the table at your book signing, can be passed out to friends and family, co-workers and strangers. It's a visual reminder about you and your book.

And it's cheap advertising.

Go for it.

For more on how to self-publish properly, please see my book, GETTING DOWN AND DIGITAL: HOW TO SELF-PUBLISH YOUR BOOK. http://amzn.to/1eBljN5

And . . .

Axiom-man & Redsaw go head-to-head in this superhero thriller & open a doorway to an evil world DOORWAY OF DARKNESS http://amzn.to/1hMg1o1

End transmission.

Issue Twenty-seven - November 8, 2014

This newsletter is meant for sharing. Tell someone.

Welcome.

It's Tuesday for me, but will be Saturday when you read this.

27.1

Comic con was a huge success. I sold a ton of books and met some great people and re-connected with others. Being somewhat of a hermit, comic con is a chance for me to catch up with folks I know in the creative community in person, talk shop and also talk life.

One of the conversations that stuck out for me was one I had with someone I used to know. This person is an incredible artist, but when I asked her if she was still drawing, she said no. It saddened me to hear this because she has such amazing talent. I then found out it was her inner critic that was keeping her down, something I can fully sympathize with. At the same time, I have a thing against inner critics because they have a knack for stopping someone from reaching their full potential. I know I struggle with that inner critic when it comes to my artwork. I know I'm not the worst artist in the world, but I also know my stuff doesn't measure up when compared to the likes of others. I want to share with you how I deal with it in case you're having a battle with your own inner critic.

First thing I do is put things into perspective. Like that grand piece of wisdom I heard another author tell me about our books, it applies here: it's *only* a book. In this case, it's *only* a drawing. Kingdoms aren't going to rise and fall over what you create. It's simply a drawing and whether good or bad, that's all it is. I'm not saying don't take it seriously, but what I am say is not to make a big deal out of it.

I then remember why I do take the time to draw. Simply put: I like doing it. That's reason enough on its own to hunker down at the drawing board and turn out a picture. If you enjoy doing something creative, do it for the pleasure of it. That's enough reward on its own: the joy you get from doing something you love.

Another thing: surround yourself with people who'll build you up instead of tear you down. Hang out and talk with other creative people, those who inspire you to get working on your latest project. Read their blogs, their tweets, their Facebook updates, view their art—soak up as much inspiration as you can. Soon you won't be able to help yourself but get started.

Talk positive to yourself and override the voice inside that tells you you can't do it or your stuff isn't good enough. You know what? Yeah, it might not be perfect or the greatest thing ever created, but if it comes from within you, from that honest place inside your heart, then what you create immediately has value and you should recognize that.

Look at creating as an opportunity to grow. I look back on my books and my first one was a doozy. Good story, but awful writing. Ever since then I've tried to do myself one better with each outing. The same applies to your art. Have a problem drawing people's heads crooked? That's okay. Draw the picture then work on straightening them out on the next one. Still slightly crooked? No problem. Try again and keep going.

Every picture—or block of writing—doesn't need to be the *Mona Lisa* or *War and Peace*. What it does need to be, though, is an expression of your inner artist, *not* your inner critic. If you can pull that off, then you've really accomplished something.

At the end of it all, just do it because you enjoy it. You can only get better with practice, but you can't practice without doing it.

Final point: a friend of mine is a talented artist, but he always seemed to have it on the backburner and never really tried to do something with his art.

Now he has and he's a regular at the cons. He even does more cons than I do. He gets commissions, freelance work, and his art just keeps getting better. But none of that would've happened unless he simply got down to business and started giving his art a chance.

There's a lesson in this.

Listen.

27.2

Got some work done on the graphic novel while at the con. Was finally able to get the opening page going. Unfortunately, I forgot my outline at home so had to go off of memory and was only able to take it so far without finding myself going down a rabbit hole, one that hadn't already been pre-determined. Needless to say, I got the thing started and I plan on fleshing out the outline more this week as I want this thing scripted and ready for the drawing stage as soon as possible.

I'll give you the title of what I hope will be a series of graphic novels: *Fox*, named after the main character.

The planned subtitle for this particular story is *Tent Girl.*

More as this develops.

27.3

My birthday is coming up next week and the Mrs. asked me what I wanted. I told her I wanted a copy of *Batman: Assault on Arkham*, which is an animated Bat-flick that takes place in the same universe as the Batman *Arkham* video games. I haven't seen it yet, but know it's a must-have for my superhero movie shelf. Earlier today I realized that maybe I should have asked for *Arrow* Season Two, as I haven't seen that either thanks to not having cable. Oh well. My wife reads these newsletters so this is just me giving her another idea.

Speaking of not having cable, I still don't have it even though I said I might get it in the fall. Starting to get a hankering for it as I miss my Food Network and have been hearing nothing but good things about *Gotham* and *The Flash.*

We'll see.

27.4

As mentioned, comic con was a huge success. One of the things that I know contributed to this was my display. I went vertical this year instead of horizontal and on either end of my table I had re-purposed shoe racks with dollar store baskets connected to them with zip ties. This created display racks in which I was able to showcase my books. Between these two racks I had more books on the table with some of them up on stands to highlight them, with my new one, *Mech Apocalypse*, in the middle. Behind me I had my Axiom-man banner. I needed to stand out amongst the many artists tabling there and by going vertical, I created something eye-catching.

That's my marketing tip this week: take time to design a good display for your books.

I've seen amazing displays complete with book stands and posters, a nice tablecloth, props, and bold and clear signage—and I've also seen the artist with next to nothing on the table other than their stuff spread out. No tablecloth, even.

Think about it: you're creating a storefront for a weekend—even a day—and customers like attractive displays, not something that looks like it belongs in a yard sale.

Get a piece of paper and sit down and draw out your set up. You don't have to plan the exact spot where each of your titles will go, but it would be good to mark out where your books will be laid out, your stands, your signage and come up with a design that's pleasing to the eye, a display that would attract *you.* If you're attracted to it, odds are others will be as well.

If it's your first show, you don't have to go all out, but at the very least bring a tablecloth, some book stands—picture stands work well for this—and clear signs with a catchy headline and some pricing info.

If it's your second or third show, go a little bigger and bring some posters of your book cover(s). Get a banner with your name or a character of yours on it. Have a lot of books? Consider forgoing the small display stands and get something bigger to accommodate all your titles.

Make a display that draws people in, not one that people look at and go, "Oh, that's nice," and move on.

Food for thought.

Something else to think about . . .

Suddenly sucked into a parallel world, Axiom-man finds himself fighting against the ravenous undead in THE DEAD LAND
http://amzn.to/hhuLsT

End transmission.

Issue Twenty-eight - November 15, 2014

So . . . we meet again.

Read this, because I made it for you.

It's Tuesday again as I write this.

28.1

Last week I talked about soaking up inspiration to motivate you to draw/write/etc.

I have lots of sources and one of them is a comics-making chap named John Porcellino. Before my site shut down earlier this year, I had written an article about his book, *King-Cat Classix*, and posted it. I found the lost post via the Internet Archive and want to preserve it here.

This is it as it was posted:

John Porcellino is a legend in the indie comic/minicomic/zine world. His autobiographical comic book, *King-Cat Comix and Stories*, is a staple in the minicomic community and he's been doing it since 1989. Issue 74, recently released, is the latest one.

The book in the pics is *King-Cat Classix*, which collects the best stories from the early issues of the series. Some of the stories in it are autobiographical, others are made up. Nowadays, John sticks to autobio, but these early stories show a vivid imagination and someone who is working their way through life through the good times and bad. It's an extremely authentic book. I have the follow-up, *Map of my Heart*, too, but that's for another entry.

John's comics are an important part of my graphic novel collection. I found him on the Net when I was checking to see if anyone published zines fulltime. It was *King-Cat* and Alec Longstreth's *Phase 7* and Julia Wertz's *Fart Party* that inspired my own *Canister X Comix*. Unfortunately, with my book writing and tying up loose ends for Coscom Entertainment, my time to make comics is nil. Hopefully this year.

Back to *King-Cat.* John's stories are extremely down-to-earth. Some are about profound moments in his life, others are just about, well, life. And that's the thing about life, isn't it? It has its moments where things are really amazing, others where it's just whatever, and yet others where things suck so bad you wish you were never born. What a thing.

From a creator standpoint, what intrigues me about John Porcellino and *King-Cat Comix and Stories* is that, so far as I know, minicomics are John's fulltime job along with running the Spit and a Half Distro. The man's a machine and tours zine and indie comic conventions like crazy to push his books and those he carries. You can read about his adventures on his blog.

I find it incredibly inspiring and motivating.

Thanks, John.

28.2

Last Friday, the 7th, I went to the coffee shop and brought my notebook and outline for *Fox.* I turned out 10 pages of comic script while following the outline. Like I've said, I've never outlined before so it's refreshing to try writing from a different angle. It's still too early in the process to see if outlining hinders the creative flow. I know that if I had outlined a novel, I'd find it frustrating, but so far outlining seems to be working for scripting comics.

I hope to have another coffee shop date soon to get more work done. Sure, I can do it from home, but the coffee shop is a special writing place for me as I once wrote an entire book there and used to almost live there when not writing way back in the day. Feels good to kind of recreate that.

Also getting ideas for more books and stories, but am trying to stick to my current project list as per the newsletter from a couple weeks back. Only so many hours in the day.

28.3

I'm missing comic con right now. It's such a magical time and I had a blast and a half this year. Did really well at the show on a professional level, but also had a great time personally while hanging out with friends. It's so cool when you can get together with a group of people who are on the same wavelength as you. It's hard being a mild-mannered citizen outside the con (not that I am; I flaunt my geekiness pretty much every chance I get. I made a decision a long time ago to not be ashamed of it), so geeking out with others is a treasure to me.

Been looking a bit at my con schedule for next year. There are some smaller shows outside the big one but the table fees have tripled and, as per this year's experience doing the small shows, it wouldn't be worth it to pay for just a one-day show. I might cave and do one as an experiment, but at the same time I don't want to lose any money either. Though, truth be told, I'd be fine with breaking even as I have such a good time at these things anyway. Maybe I'll go halfers on a table with someone?

Time'll tell.

Also scheduled a book signing for later this year at Coles Bookstore in Kildonan Place on December 21 at noon. If you're in the Winnipeg area, come down and say hi.

28.4

I want to talk a little about book printers and the principles here apply to novels or comics. In short, choosing a printer is about planning as you basically have two choices when it comes to book printing: printing on-demand or printing offset. The former is when you print a book(s) when needed, the latter is printing a ton of copies at once and then possibly going back to press at a later date.

The advantage to printing on-demand is you only print books when required and in smaller quantities. This helps you not to spend a ton of cash up front and risk not recovering it. The disadvantage is printing on-demand means you pay more per book printed than you would via offset printing thus reducing your per-book profit.

Here's the point: you need to forecast your sales before choosing a printer. What I mean is if you know that the book is only going to sell a little bit or at a steady stream, going on-demand would be the better choice and I can't recommend my printer, Lightning Source, highly enough. (For more on Lightning Source and why they're the best in cost and distribution, see my book *Getting Down and Digital: How to Self-publish Your Book* here: http://amzn.to/1eBljN5)

If you know you're going to have a lot of upfront sales (i.e. a distributor is going to place a decent-sized order, you got some pre-order sales, some events planned and a means to sell through a lot of stock), then going offset in a reasonable quantity would be a better choice because the more you print in one shot, the cheaper your per-unit cost is going to be thus increasing your per-book profit.

You can also do a hybrid approach and have a company like Lightning Source in place to handle all your on-line sales via their automated methods, and then go offset to fulfill a large order from, say, Diamond Distributors.

When choosing an offset printer, I would recommend seeing a sample finished book from them and getting familiar with the paper types, cover stocks, finishes, etc. and then choosing from those what options are best cost-wise for your book and your goals.

All I can caution against is not getting carried away in quantity printing. Print what you need and maybe a little bit over for "down the road" sales. The last thing you want is to be sitting on 3,000 books and them not moving. I also suggest printing locally if possible to save on shipping.

Usually in this day and age of digital publishing, printing on-demand is the recommended choice, however, there are exceptions and I want you to be aware of that.

I also want you to be aware of this:

The city is covered in a black cloud and a new supervillain has taken over. Axiom-man battles it out in CITY OF RUIN http://amzn.to/1gxybUM

End transmission.

Issue Twenty-nine - November 23, 2014

Thank you for subscribing to *The Canister X Transmission*, where we broadcast this newsletter weekly from a secret base in Winnipeg, Manitoba.

29.1

I'm fortunate because, unlike most artists, my whole family is artistic. I do books and comics, my wife makes comics, and my kids make stories and comics. We could totally form a company and give DC and Marvel a run for their money. But, like all artists, we run into trouble now and then and sometimes the ideas and stories don't flow as well as we would like.

My wife is a gifted cartoonist. She's done three books so far: *Fuzz Society* Nos. 1 and 2 and a 24-hour comic called *Average Jill*. Half of *Fuzz Society* No. 3 is sitting on her drawing table but, you see, she's hit a snag and she's given me permission to talk about it here. Her problem is that she's an artist and not a storyteller. Her art flows from her fingers no problem when she knows what to draw, but the dam builds up when she hits a mental block and that block is what's preventing her from completing this latest issue. She's wrapped up the current plots in *Fuzz Society* and is ready to start a new one(s) except she doesn't know what to write.

Some would call this writer's block. I've dealt with this beast before way back when I was working on my first book. I was "blocked" for two months before getting back to finishing the story. I knew where the story was headed but didn't know how to bridge the gap between where I was and where I was going.

Nowadays, I personally don't believe in writer's block. I think writer's block is more a result of a few triggers. One of them is being overwhelmed by writing a story. Sometimes writing can be daunting, especially if your story is large in scope. It's easy to get wrapped up in the *size* of it rather than letting your brain work it out for itself. My cure for this is to tackle the story in little chunks. Yes, it's going to be big when it's done, but you don't have to write big to make it big. Take each chapter bit by bit. Take each scene bit by bit. Even take each paragraph bit by bit and handle the story in little steps instead of giant leaps. Seems to help me, anyway.

Was talking to another writer and they said distraction is another component of writer's block. Sometimes our heads get full of either all the elements of our story or just with life stuff in general. This is where discipline comes in. Turn off the Internet, go to a quiet corner of the house—leave the house if you have to and hit the coffee shop—turn off the music (or put headphones on and use the music to block out mental distraction), and get to work. Our brains are funny. It seems like they either hyper focus on a particular task or we think of so many things at once we can't get a foothold on anything. Whatever's going through your head—those issues—aren't going to change any more or any less if you just shove them aside for half an hour so you can write. It's like staying awake at night and thinking of everything you have to do the next day. It's a waste of time. Those things aren't going to get done by thinking of them so it's best to just turn your brain off and go to sleep. Same for writing. Turn those thoughts—even feelings—off and just concentrate on the work for half an hour or for 500 words or whatever.

The last thing is you can be stuck for ideas. I'm a proponent of the story feeding itself, with each element in the story giving birth to the next element, however, sometimes the ideas won't come. This is where I've found using life experience as a go-to source to be helpful. There's an old saying: write what you know. And what do we know best? Our own lives. Even if your story is a sci-fi in outer space with weird space creatures, though you haven't experienced that personally, you can still invest yourself into your character. Give them something to overcome that you've overcome. Have them react to seeing a space monster the same way you'd react. Does your character have a goal? If not, give them one of your own and relive your experiences through them. Soon you'll find the story telling itself because you've already been there.

Again, the main thing is not to get overwhelmed. Like I've been preaching, at the end of the day, it's just a story. It's not life or death. Just write—good or bad—and have fun. The work will get done if you don't obsess over it. It'll be a lot more pleasant, too. And even if you think you botched it up, when you go over for rewrites later, you'll see that usually what you wrote isn't that bad after all.

29.2

Work is progressing nicely on the *Fox* graphic novel. I'm writing page 40-something as of today (Wednesday). I'm about a quarter through the book as I estimate it'll be around 150 pages when done. Once completed, I'll go over the script and make adjustments where necessary then it's off to the drawing board for character and set designs.

Feels good to be working on comics again.

29.3

It was my birthday recently so I went ahead and hit Amazon.ca and ordered up some graphic novels. I ordered *Kane* Vols. 1 and 2 by Paul Grist and *The Hospital Suite* by John Porcellino (see last newsletter for my write-up about him). Really looking forward to jumping into these. Estimated delivery date is Dec. 5-15.

Been busy reading Frank Miller's *Sin City* in the meantime and so far have re-read *Sin City, That Yellow Bastard,* and am currently reading *Family Values.* Frank's black and white artwork is amazing and I'm finding his books a good source of artistic inspiration.

29.4

Hardcovers. Are they important?

To me, the answer is yes and no. Most of the big name authors get a release in hardcover first then a paperback follows. For the indie author, it's basically paperbacks and eBooks. A big reason is the price to our readers because hardcovers cost more to produce. The question is, should the indie author include hardcovers in their publication plan? They could. They don't have to. But they could. You don't need to do the "big name" thing and release in hardcover and eBook first then go do a paperback. You could instead release in all three formats simultaneously so that readers who prefer whatever format have an option.

Personally, I like hardcovers and if I was made of money they'd be the only books I'd buy. Alas, I'm not, so have both hardcovers and paperbacks in my collection.

Anyway . . .

In the age of digital and on-demand publishing, including a hardcover version of your book is pretty straightforward. The interior would be the same as the interior of your paperback—just with a different ISBN number because it's a different format—and only the cover layout would change. You could use the same image, but then create the art/layout for the dust jacket's inside flaps. The only cost is the time it takes to create it, that's it. Oh, and the distribution fee to keep it available to the general public.

The idea here is keeping options open for your readers. Besides, there's something prestigious about having a hardcover release while everyone is doing paperbacks. Might elevate your reputation a little.

You can also do the limited edition thing and make your book available as a collector's hardcover, limited to, say, 100 copies or something, all signed and numbered. Because it's limited, you can ask for $40-50 each even if they cost you $15 or so per unit to print. Not a bad payday, assuming you sell them all.

In the end, going hardcover is a way to make your book available in all three reading formats.

You can even make a large print edition, but that's a discussion for another time.

A question:

What happens when a young girl versed in kung fu takes Axiom-man on a jaunt throughout the city? Find out in UNDERGROUND CRUSADE. http://amzn.to/1m0aHL5

End transmission.

Issue Thirty - November 29, 2014

Welcome to *The Canister X Transmission*, where we discuss the creative life week-to-week and talk about it without fear of going to less than desirable places.

This is also Issue Thirty. A nice round number.

Enjoy.

30.1

I'm in deep trouble. Serious trouble. I just resurrected an old idea and it's something to the tune of ten books. Kid's books, but books nonetheless. And the stories are talking. I have the first one pretty much mapped out and the titles—hence what they're about—of the nine others planned. It ties in with *The Axiom-man Saga*, though can be read completely independently of it and, of course, is for a different age group.

Add those to my list of projects.

Don't have enough time.

Time to buckle down and get serious. Thinking of entering a winter hibernation mode where all I do is write. Really crank the stuff out so I can stay on schedule.

These are dribbles of thoughts, really, and I'm sharing them with you because this newsletter is my only long-winded conduit to the world. My website is there as a kind of placeholder on the Web.

Recently got sucked into checking Facebook regularly which is something I'm thinking of stepping back on so I can work without the social media world hovering in the back of my mind. Might streamline to just this newsletter and Twitter until I can get these projects wrapped up.

I think of the New Year and all that I have to get done, all the things left undone, all the things that are as yet unformed in my mind that will no doubt creep up on me.

Busy.

30.2

Working on *Fox*. It's Wednesday as I type this. Have a work date at the coffee shop tomorrow night. Will churn out some pages. With my overload of projects, am wondering if I'll actually have the time to draw the graphic novel or if I'll have to get an artist.

Decisions.

30.3

Bat in the Sun Productions just released their latest Super Power Beat Down. This one was Batman vs Darth Vader. Utterly amazing. The attention to detail was astounding, everything from the Death Star to the Batwing, the costumes to the actors, the effects to the story. It ended perfectly, too. If *The Axiom-man Saga* was ever made into a movie, Bat in the Sun would be the company I would trust with it.

Prepare to have your life changed: http://youtu.be/nj23dwWHukY

Stunning.

30.4

Can I trust you?

It's a question that is asked of every author. Can you be trusted to deliver a good book?

See, publishing sucks right now. That's being honest. Every Tom, Dick and Harry has a book out thanks to the ease of self-publishing and, to be honest, many of them are not that good. Many of them are by writers who are still learning their craft but have gone along and published their story or book even though said story or book wasn't ready to be published. Joe Reader comes along and buys this book because it sounds interesting and is sadly disappointed in the end by poor writing.

Can I trust you?

Does your book stand up? Is it your first? Are you just writing whatever and sending it out into the ether hoping for some quick cash? Did you take the time to learn how to write properly before doing so?

Readers are tired of wading through garbage to find the diamonds in the rough. They're tired of buying cheap eBooks because most of them are a let-down in the end. They're going back to sticking with authors they recognize, ones they know who'll deliver a good story and solid writing.

Are you pouring yourself into your work? Or are you just calling it "good enough" and walking away? Do you even care about what the readers will think or are you just so excited to have a book out that you'll publish yours despite its flaws?

Can I trust you?

Will you become an author I recognize?

A writer doesn't need to publish everything they write just because they can no differently than an artist doesn't put up for sale everything they draw. Unfortunately, we've been brainwashed to think otherwise thanks to all the Kindle hype and this "publishing revolution" nonsense.

You need to write a good book, one that's objectively good and isn't just "good" because you or your mom think so.

If this is your first time doing this, get some people other than your friends to read it and tell you what they think. And, no, don't give it to a bunch of other writers whose only purpose is to scratch the other guy's back and make them feel good. Find a readers group and offer it there. People who are junkies for the printed word will offer up opinions far more valuable than a bunch of other start-up writers who only know how to glad-hand.

Can I trust you?

Can you convince me your book is worth my money and time? Is it so good that I'll buy your next one because you've earned my trust with your first?

Questions.

Please tell others about this newsletter. The link you can give them is http://www.tinyletter.com/apfuchs You can also visit that link to read back issues in case you're just joining us.

Ad:

End transmission.

Issue Thirty-one - December 6, 2014

Welcome, my pretties. Follow this Yellow Brick Road to insight.

We're not in Kansas anymore.

31.1

Made a choice this past week and that was to step away from social media and the Web for a while. The reason is I have so many deadlines that I need to clear up some headspace for them instead of having my "web responsibilities" lurking in the back of my mind. So with that, I've entered winter hibernation mode with my main conduits to the world being this newsletter and private email. Even for the latter, I only plan on checking it every other day.

I think it's healthy for writers—or any creator—to do this and just simply be alone with their project(s). Now I can put my undivided attention on what I need to do without trying to keep up with the lives of others or trying to entertain others with my own. Sounds selfish, but the priority has always been the work and with, frankly, Facebook being a lousy way to market your work, I'm not missing out on anything. Even Twitter is losing its pull in terms of being a place to market books. Right now, they're good for keeping folks up to date on what's going on or simply to share items of interest as opposed to just being a place for ads for your latest title.

That's why I have this newsletter. I can keep you guys up to date with what's going on in my creative life while also, at the end of each newsletter, let you know about a book of mine. I get to both engage with you and market something without having to do so daily because this newsletter only goes out once a week.

That's not to say I have an issue with engaging with people regularly on Facebook or Twitter, but rather simply there are times when that stuff needs to get turned off in order to complete tasks waiting to be done. It's just like taking a break from TV. No harm in it. I'm not going to be gone forever. I'll back in a few weeks or early in the New Year and things'll be right as rain again.

And, again, this newsletter will keep on going so I haven't disappeared completely.

31.2

On the work progress front, I'm still plugging away on *Fox* and I'm nearly at the halfway point of the graphic novel. Real happy about that. It's also turning out to be a bigger story than I expected in terms of how many pages it's taking to convey my ideas, story mood, panel pacing, etc.

It's Tuesday right now and yesterday I started up that kid's series I mentioned last newsletter so the first story is roughly a third done. I hope to finish it this week then make some decisions in terms of illustration and publication. The main thing is to get the story out so that comes first.

Saturday update: I finished the kids book and also its second draft. The next step is to do third draft. I also talked with an artist this week and he's going to take a crack at doing the illustrations for the book once the third draft is ready, which will be soon.

31.3

In the big world of fandom, Star Wars fans were recently given the teaser trailer for *Star Wars: The Force Awakens.* I loved it, like a good fanboy should. And it was indeed a teaser. It showed just enough to get you excited about a new Star Wars movie without showing anything storywise. Okay, okay, they did show that sith with the lightsaber. Speaking of which, many folks are kicking up a fuss about the crossguard on the saber, which is made from mini lightsabers. Personally, I thought it was an interesting take on the weapon. My only concern is the user of it will have to hold it carefully lest one wrong move causes the guards to slice their forearms or somewhere else on their person.

The other thing people made an issue about—and I couldn't believe it—was the black stormtrooper at the beginning of the trailer. And I'm talking black in terms of skin color, not armor color. I didn't even notice it until people started pointing it out. It only makes sense that in a *galaxy* far, far away there would be a racially-diverse group of people and some of them would want to be stormtroopers. We know black people exist in the Star Wars universe—i.e. Lando Calrissian—so I don't see the big deal here.

Anyway . . . here's a link to the trailer: http://youtu.be/OMOVFvcNfvE

31.4

Author branding. I hate that term. I really do. To me it cheapens the artist and makes them a product versus a creator, but given the commercialistic society we live in, that's how we do things so it only makes sense it would creep its way into how we make books.

There are a lot of aspects to author branding but today I'm going to focus on book covers. While I know a lot of book covers tend to look the same these days, have you noticed that if an author has more than one book out there's a continuity between their book covers, everything between the font for the title and the font for their name? Even the images used tend to have a common thread between titles. This is done to set that author apart from all the others in the store. It's meant to draw your eye so when you see that book in that style you know you're getting Joe Author's book instead of someone else's. James Patterson is a good example of this. His book covers all look the same with those big block letters on them. Mary Higgins Clark also has a consistent look to her books. Same with Danielle Steel.

Now what does this mean for you? It means that, especially if you're doing a series, you should have a common thread between your book covers, both in the images and in the text.

What if you're like me and have multiple series across multiple genres? Well, I could pull a James Patterson and make them all look the same, but what I opted for was the same text and art style for each series because each series has its own vibe. This sets each series apart while still letting the reader know they belong to each other. It also looks nice on the shelf.

Next time you're at the bookstore, browse the aisles and when you see an author who has multiple titles, pull them out and compare the covers. This might give you ideas as to what to do with your own.

This is one way to brand yourself amidst the millions of books out there and make yourself stand out.

I wrote a book under a pen name once:

Two people. One weekend. Love. Sometimes people get to you, underneath, where it counts, in APRIL by Peter Fox
http://amzn.to/cObrh7

End transmission.

Issue Thirty-two - December 13, 2014

Broadcasting from winter hibernation, this is *The Canister X Transmission.*

This issue is brought to you by the letter A and the number 7 and the color blue.

32.1

Things are getting worse. I mean it. I have too much to do and not enough time to do it in. Scratch that: I have the time, but I can't write straight for eight hours a day. My brain doesn't sustain that kind of creative output. It needs downtime to recharge. True, I do have the brain power to sustain eight hours a day of new *ideas*, but I don't have the strength to take those ideas and transform them into coherent thoughts and sentences for that kind of duration.

And yet my to-do list is incredibly full as per a few newsletters back.

Here's what you do if you're in the same boat: keep working, even if it's not for eight hours a day. Chip away at the projects and get them done. Do something every day even if it's just a little bit. If you're on a deadline, then you'll need to break it down into the required chunks needed to make that deadline. Have the first draft of an 80,000-word novel due in a month? Then you gotta do 2,667 words a day to make deadline. Have less to do? Adjust accordingly.

We're in a "getting things done" phase over here. With social media turned off for the most part, I'm able to focus on getting done what needs doing. Face it: we live in a world of distraction so if you can control some of those distracting variables, might as well go for it.

Today—Thursday—I finished taking the kid's book as far as I could go at this stage. Now it's with the artist. We're aiming for a release in January sometime. My next task for today is to do the first draft of this newsletter, which will be collected in book form around June 2015. I'm getting that done. After I'm done this, I'm writing a letter so I have more content for *Canadian Scribbler: Collected Letters of an Underground Writer Vol. 2*. That'll take me to the end of the working day.

It's all about getting things done and not simply thinking about getting things done. It's easy—because I've done it—to let weeks go by without producing anything . . . and then scrambling come deadline, or missing a deadline completely as a result. Like I've told many people, books don't write themselves. There needs to be a writer actually writing behind them.

If you're lagging behind or haven't written in a while and have a lot to do, why not start cracking down on things today? Take some time and actually write. You'll feel better afterwards, and the sense of accomplishment once you're done is tremendously rewarding.

32.2

This past week I didn't work on the *Fox* graphic novel and instead focused on getting my kid's book ready. I did my third draft and then went back over it again and inserted drawing instructions for the artist where appropriate. I even took the time to format the bulk of the book so I knew more or less where everything went layout-wise.

Like I just mentioned, I'm aiming to get the book out in January, with the second book—which I started—to follow shortly after. The ideal would be to release one a month for six months straight, but we'll see what the artist's schedule is like first.

Before the year is out I'd like to have the first draft of the script for *Fox* done. After that, I'm going to finish up *Mech Apocalypse 2* and *Robot City*. I plan to release those sometime within the first half of 2015.

32.3

Shooting on *Batman v Superman* has wrapped. I'm pleased. The sooner they get it done, the better, but I don't know the extent of the post-production work required for the flick so who knows when they'll actually be done-done. This movie isn't due out until early 2016. I'm hoping that if they finish things sooner than expected, they might possibly bump the date even more and give us a Christmas 2015 release. Roughly a year and half from now is still a long time to wait for this movie. Rumor has it a teaser trailer will be out before the year is done, possibly attached to the final *Hobbit* movie.

I'm also excited for the toy lineup for the flick as I collect Superman action figures. Here's hoping they have a slick version of the Man of Steel planned for the toy line.

32.4

Today we're going to talk about choosing a trim size for your book. If you're doing comics, then you have no choice but to choose a trim size that is either industry standard or something slightly bigger (manga books aside). For example, you can fit an industry standard-sized page on an 8.5" x 11" piece of paper, like how Dave Sim did when he released the *Cerebus* trade paperbacks.

For novels, choosing a trim size is important because not only does it change the overall presentation of your book, it also determines how much money you'll make per unit because the smaller the trim size, the more pages your book will be, thus increasing your printing costs.

Most indie authors publish a standard 6" x 9" paperback. I do, too, for books of mine that are standard length of 70,000 words and up. This enables me to get as many words on the page without making the book physically too big.

But what do you do for shorter works? Should you go with a 6" x 9" anyway? You can, but this will also result in a slimmer book, one that might look a little strange being so big dimension-wise but very thin in terms of thickness.

This is where choosing a smaller trim size comes in handy. Going down to a 5.5" x 8.5" or 5" x 8" book will add heft to your finished product because the page count will increase.

As said, there's a trade-off: the more pages your book is, the more it'll cost to print per unit.

At the same time, if you're going for that pocket book kind of feel, doing a smaller trim size would be in your favor as mass market paperbacks are much smaller than your average indie-produced trade paperback. (They also print them in huge quantities, which is why they can get away with a smaller book that's super thick and still charge a good price for it.)

Trim size is something to consider and I wouldn't necessarily default to the standard 6" x 9" just because everyone else is. Even going a different size could set your book apart from the slew of regular-sized books out there.

Smaller sizes are good for novellas, even novelettes.

Case in point: the first Axiom-man book is 60,000-some-odd words. Had I done it as a 6" x 9", it would've been a thin book, coming in under 200 pages. I wanted the book to have some bulk so I opted for a 5" x 8". This put the book at over 200 pages and made the reader feel they're getting good value for their dollar. On the flip side, my zombie novel, *Blood of the Dead*, is over 80,000 words, so I opted for 6" x 9" to help keep the page count down, but still deliver a big enough book that the reader feels they're getting value. Would I have made more money on a larger-dimensioned Axiom-man book? Yes, but then it'd seem I was cheating the reader. At the same time, I would've made less money per unit on *Blood of the Dead* had I gone with a smaller trim size, but since there was a certain per-unit profit I wanted to make off that book I adjusted my trim size accordingly.

Just remember that if you're doing a series, all the books in that series should be the same size regardless of each one's length. It'd look, and present, weird otherwise.

Trim sizes are something to consider as you go about the publishing process of your book. Part of the thing to consider is what you want out of it profit-wise and also what you think the reader deserves to get out of it page count-wise and what makes a nicer book in the end.

Adieu.

Sometimes a piece of Heaven comes down to you. Jack finds this out with Cyan in MY ANGEL AND ME http://amzn.to/hkuZkL

End transmission.

Issue Thirty-three - December 20, 2014

Welcome to *The Canister X Transmission.*

Web rundown:

Website: www.canisterx.com
Twitter: www.twitter.com/ap_fuchs
Facebook: www.facebook.com/apfuchsbooks
Newsletter: www.tinyletter.com/apfuchs
Pinterest: www.pinterest.com/apfuchs

Join me at the above links.

33.1

Fragments . . .

Coffee is my lifeline lately. Drinking somewhere around a pot or more a day. Seems to be the only fuel to keep me going. I like big cups, so it takes around 5 of them to finish a pot. Day doesn't get started without coffee. Day doesn't finish without it either. Trying to not drink it after 7, but it's 8:10 right now on Wednesday evening and I have a mug of the stuff sitting in front of me.

. . .

Went out for drinks with fellow writers Andrew Lorenz and Christine Steendam last night. Had a couple large beers and some nachos. Important to hang out with other writer-types. Gets me out of Hermitville. Also a chance to inspire each other, hear about each other's projects, and talk shop.

. . .

Enjoying pulling back from Facebook involvement. Not sure how much of a marketing tool it's going to be in the near future anyway. Good for just hanging out, but no longer is the place to post ads for books. Doing the "writer circuit" and posting ads for books in various reading/writing groups seems a waste of time. I never see a boost in sales because of it. Using the author page at Facebook as a broadcasting point right now. Enjoy Twitter's interaction much more.

. . .

Lots going on on the personal front as Christmas draws near. Good news is the shopping is pretty much done. The Mrs. has a few more homemade gifts to complete, but otherwise we're all set for the 25th. The only Christmas stress I need to worry about at present is what I'm bringing for food on Christmas Eve and Christmas Day. And it is a stress because I try and bring something unique to the table and not just your run-of-the-mill mashed potatoes.

. . .

Also, on a personal note, been working through some issues so things are a bit of a slog at the moment. No matter. I try and live by Harvey Pekar's words: "Every day is a brand new deal, right? Just keep on working. Something's bound to turn up."

33.2

Approximately a third of the way through the second book in my kids series. I have the next few scenes mapped out mentally. Just need to write them. Hope to finish the first draft soon so I could do some revisions and send it to the artist for production.

The hero's name is Power Jam. It'll make sense when you read it. He's eleven, in grade six. He's a challenge to write in the context he still lives at home with his parents and so everything is done under supervision. Hard to be a hero that way.

Thought: writing for kids is a good exercise in writing for a different audience than I'm used to. Writing versatility is a virtue, I think.

33.3

Arrow Season 2 arrived in the mail last week. Been watching it with the Mrs. We're enjoying it. Binge watching, to me, is where it's at. As much as I sort of enjoy the quasi-suspense of waiting a week to see what happens next, I feel my dopamine levels rising when I get to indulge in a series and take it all in at once.

Season 3, as per the Intervibes, is also turning out quite well. Might find a way to watch it after Season 2.

33.4

Part of a writer's group on Facebook. It's driving me nuts hence one of the reasons I've stepped back from social media for a season. I poked my head in the other day and the discussion was whether or not one should edit one's own work prior to publication, that is, the writer—and only the writer—gets to edit it.

The sad thing was many in the discussion agreed to not getting an outside editor for their work prior to self-publishing.

This is why self-publishing—despite its current hype—gets a bad rap: too many writers releasing unedited work.

Here's this week's tip: get an editor. Period. Even for comics. A writer cannot edit his or her own work. Yes, they can redraft it and do rewrites, but in terms of them being the final say on a manuscript, it just can't be done. Why? Because they can't see the forest from the trees and too many errors remain in the book, whether those errors are simple typos or larger issues like poorly-crafted sentences.

You need an editor.

If you can't afford one, save up for one. It's worth the money. Some are very affordable, others not. I once spent over $400 on an editor to go over my second book. What I got back was a manuscript so marked up with red that the book never saw publication it was in such rough shape. But do you know what? I learned more about writing well from that experience than from anything else I've picked up over the years.

An editor knows writing. They know the English language. They understand what writing rules need to be kept in fiction and what rules can be bent or broken. They're well-read and have written a ton of material themselves.

You need their feedback and correction on your book.

I've been using an editor for ten years and have never looked back. I recognize that my stuff—while fairly clean manuscript-wise—still needs a polish and *objective* feedback over what works and what doesn't in the manuscript.

I also need to be confident that when I publish a book, it's error-free and the reader will get something of quality.

You need an editor. It's worth repeating.

You can't edit yourself.

Don't add to the self-publishing stigma by releasing a book that has only been gone over by you. It's not worth it; not for the reader, and not for your career.

Hire someone who knows what they're doing. Be patient. Take the time to learn to write properly before publishing.

It can only serve you and the reader in the end. It'll make your book better, it'll make you better.

In other news:

Painfully tortured for his faith, God opens Duncan's eyes to the spirits responsible. It's supernatural suspense in UNDENIABLE http://amzn.to/1cowXfs

End transmission.

Issue Thirty-four - December 27, 2014

From out of the shadows comes *The Canister X Transmission*, ready to defend the lives of writers and creators everywhere.

Tune into the latest broadcast below . . .

34.1

Fragments 2 . . .

Talked with another writer recently about the pressures of the business. We hashed out some issues and in the end discovered that I need to step back from the pressure side of publishing and get back to the love of creating. See, when you first start, it's all about the love of the craft. When you start publishing, things mutate and it starts to become about a "product." Then it becomes about making more of those products. Eventually, you lose sight of why you started in the first place. I've written before about how romantic writing my first book was and how I want to get back to that kind of zone/mental space. There's a reason: I need to get back to basics because I tend to let the complexities of publishing—in all dynamics—get to me. And it's unhealthy.

. . .

Appreciating the machine that is the brain and how it pertains to creating. Have multiple streams of thought going, some creative, some business-related. These streams are currently running parallel in headspace. Occasionally they cross over and the anxieties arise. I then have to pull back and realign the thought processes so they don't intersect. Keeping things mentally compartmentalized helps streamline what can otherwise be messy thought processes. Like the saying goes, "Don't cross the streams."

. . .

Been relying on Twitter as my main source of information. I like Twitter's simplicity and how the status updates are more highlight-oriented versus the overdone/lengthy headlines and updates of

Facebook. Facebook seems like a world you can delve into and get lost in, while Twitter lets you hover above Planet Information and pick and choose where you submerge yourself. I think a part of me is having an issue with the idea that our on-line and off-line lives are merging. I remember when one's on-line life was your email, your website and maybe a newsgroup or message board. That was it. Social media has changed that and there's a crossover happening that, personally, I don't see as healthy yet, it seems, is a necessary part of life first and foremost for the artist, secondly as a non-creative individual.

. . .

It's the 23rd as I write this. Christmas Eve is tomorrow. Festivities start for me around late afternoon. I heard Santa's coming tomorrow night. Better help the kids pick the cookies as I tend to know what Santa's tastes are. Christmas Day to follow. Boxing Day after that, which hosts another Christmas dinner. Food and drink will characterize all three events.

It will be after Christmas when you get this newsletter. I hope you and yours had a wonderful time filled with laughter, family and friends, a cool gift or two and more food than you knew what to do with.

Merry Christmas. Happy New Year as well.

34.2

Half-done the second *Power Jam* book as of this writing.

Had a book signing Sunday, which went well. While there I managed to work on the *Fox* graphic novel in between signing books. It's coming together.

Also, a few days ago, I located the working draft of *Robot City*, which sits at roughly 3/4 done. *Robot City* is a reworking of the *Zomtropolis* serial novel which ran on my website but has since been removed. Since I don't do horror anymore, I'm turning it into a sci-fi. It'll be a fairly easy process to swap out the zombies for killer robots. Thought I had lost the manuscript but located a copy on the laptop. Mind put an ease now. I plan to finish writing the book after I wrap up the second in the *Power*

Jam series.

34.3

Re-reading the first six volumes of *Transmetropolitan* by Warren Ellis and Darick Robertson. There are ten in total, which means I need to order up the last four. It's an incredible series which takes a good hard look at society and comes away with some cut-to-the-heart truths about it. Of course, it's also appealing because it's about Spider Jerusalem, a gonzo journalist that perpetually smokes. I see a lot of myself in Spider. I'm just not as famous. While rude and crude in parts, it's a series well worth exploring for those who like comics that make you think.

Thinking comics . . . what a concept.

34.4

Most of my weekly publishing/marketing posts have been specific in terms of dealing with a set topic. This week is going to be an "overview" post about cultivating success for you and your book. Due to space constraints, I'm going to keep it simple.

Authors look at other authors and ask why some are more successful than others. They're always trying to find out that "one secret thing" the other author is doing that makes them successful.

Let's cut to it right now: there is no "one secret thing."

Success as an author comes from doing a lot of things and doing them well.

When it comes to the book itself—and this applies to comics—the author writes a good book. They have an editor. They hire a cover designer. They layout their book professionally. In the end, they put out a good product. (I know, I hate the P-word, too.) They didn't cut corners because they couldn't afford it, or didn't hire an editor because they didn't want outside eyes messing with their work. They produced the book like a professional press would instead.

Once you have the professional product, then the next step is to tell people about it.

Writers these days seem so pigeonholed in all this "upload and go" Kindle nonsense and focusing their sales solely on Amazon while ignoring or not giving priority to other sales channels. While Amazon is a heavy hitter and should not be ignored, I don't think a writer should put all their eggs in the Amazon basket. Use other sales channels. Ensure your book is available in paperback, too. Push sales to Barnes and Noble, Kobo or Smashwords. Utilize as many sales channels as you can and promote each one. This includes doing off-line sales like book signings, conventions, trunk-of-car sales. Don't just focus on all this on-line stuff.

Get the word out. You need to cast a wide net in the loud place that is the World Wide Web. Have a website, have a Facebook page, use Twitter, use Google +, use Instagram, use LinkedIn. You don't need to have your finger in every social media pie, but you need to have a presence in several and feed each social media outlet with regular content. Don't just spam each one with links to your book(s), but use them to interact with people. Post about your day, post an interesting quote, post a link to an informative article. Retweet other people's tweets. Share some statuses. Yes, it can be a lot of work, but if you delegate 10-15 minutes a day to it, that's all you need. Then you can get back to writing. The idea here is to build awareness about you and your work where people gather. Show them you as a person and they'll be apt to check out your work eventually.

Last, use other promo methods as suggested in this newsletter and outside sources. Use business cards, fliers, brochures, word-of-mouth, book reviews, guest blogging and more.

It's the mixture of all these ingredients that will one day lead to success. It's not just one thing.

Actually, there is an exception. Sometimes writers get lucky and something hits and hits big. But that's rare. Success is cumulative nine times out of ten. It's doing all the little things and putting them together into one big picture that makes all the difference.

What about you? What are you doing? Are you just picking at things here and there or are you going whole hog?

Something to think about.

For more self-publishing info and a step-by-step guide that walks you through the whole process, please check out GETTING DOWN AND DIGITAL: HOW TO SELF-PUBLISH YOUR BOOK http://amzn.to/1eBljN5

End transmission.

Issue Thirty-five - January 3, 2015

Welcome to the first issue of *The Canister X Transmission* for 2015. This year is the future according to *Back to the Future II.*

Still waiting on those hover-boards, though.

35.1

It's Wednesday, December 31st as I write this. It's time to look back on the year and go over the hopes for 2015.

2015.

Wow. Didn't think I'd make it this long but here we are.

2014 was a year of ups and downs. It started off all right, then in February I had my meltdown and shut off nearly all aspects of my life, including writing and publishing. I dismantled my business and in a bittersweet way got to experience the euphoria of starting over. A few months later I returned to publishing, unable to stay away. During that time without it, I felt like I had no direction and no purpose and got to experience the exciting fear of a fresh start. But, like I said, I couldn't stay away so have since been working on rebuilding what I destroyed, albeit to a different blueprint.

Had a relapse on the depression and anxiety front. After being over a year off medication I had to go back on it lest things fell apart even worse. Still working through that.

Learned some things about myself. Got rid of some bad habits, resurrected an old one and learned to keep my life as simple as possible. I'm definitely a different person now than I was when the year started.

I don't know what 2015 holds. I hope it holds good things, but have learned to take life one day at a time so I'll see what comes down the pike. I know I have some personal issues that need working out and I hope 2015 is the year to do it.

On the writing front, I have several projects I want to see completed and published, a mixture of fiction, non-fiction and children's fiction. Oh, some comic stuff, too.

I think my main publishing goal for 2015 is simply to have fun, though. That's all I really want in the end and that's what, for me, all this creative endeavour stuff has been about: having fun.

All other aspirations have fallen by the wayside. I'm no longer after money or fame or "a breakout hit" or any of that nonsense.

Just want to do this and have fun doing so, that's all.

35.2

Not much to report on work updates. Been working on *Fox* and getting that done. I missed my end-of-year deadline for that, unfortunately. Not much has changed since last week. All the Holiday celebration has put a good chunk of creative work on hold.

I'm sure I'm not the only writer in that boat.

35.3

I got a Superman book for Christmas. It's basically a Man of Steel encyclopedia, covering his comic book history and all his major storylines from *Action Comics* No. 1 through to the present. It's an exciting and informative read. Of course I know Superman mythology fairly well, but I'm getting tidbits of info that I wasn't aware of before and it's interesting to see how, as the comic book history is presented, it's all been one giant story since day one.

Near done reading that book, then it's back to Christine Steendam's *Heart Like an Ocean*.

35.4

Twitter's an interesting marketing tool for books and there are a bunch of ways to use it and, I'm learning, it's a social media tool with not just one set method to sell books.

Like all social media, you can't just tweet "buy my book" links and call it good. You need to actually post interesting/amusing items. Of course, feel free to pepper your tweets with [automated] "buy my book" ads, but don't make those ads your focus. Tweet about your day, retweet other tweets you find interesting, crack a joke, reply to other people's tweets, thank people for retweeting your tweets, etc.

Basically what you want to do is create a relationship between you and your followers that's both fun and interesting. Get them hooked on you as a person and it'll be much easier to turn them into customers later.

In terms of followers, we all dream of having a million of them, but that's hard to achieve. There are different ways to up your follower count on Twitter, though.

The basics:

- post your Twitter link on your website, your Facebook page, your business cards, your newsletter, anywhere you can advertise links

- write tweets of interest; by doing this, you're more apt to get retweeted thus exposing you to a bigger audience and in turn increasing your chances of being followed by new people

- a lot of people "follow back" on Twitter so what you want to do is follow people of interest and like-mindedness in the hopes they'll follow you, too. Search out particular keywords using the search feature on Twitter. i.e. "science fiction" or "kindle," and then follow those Twitter users who tweet about those keywords. A percentage of them will follow you back, thus increasing your follower count. That's basically how it's done and why you see some people with huge Twitter bases. They take time each day to grow their list. Later, you can use on-line tools like www.justunfollow.com to stop following those who aren't following you. And then the cycle continues.

(You can also use Just Unfollow to search those keywords, too, and follow new people. Actually, it's a pretty good free on-line tool. You can also upgrade to a paid version.)

The main thing with Twitter is the interaction. Join in on the conversations, post comments that are interesting and have fun socializing. Do that, then it's to your advantage when you tweet about your books.

Also, be sure you're following me on Twitter. I'm at www.twitter.com/ap_fuchs

A commercial:

Love superhero movies? Check out the ONLY superhero movie review book out there. 100 reviews. LOOK, UP ON THE SCREEN! http://amzn.to/1jVxY31

End transmission.

Issue Thirty-six - January 10, 2015

Another week, another dollar.

Here's the new issue of *The Canister X Transmission.*

36.1

So a friend in the business shoots me an email and asks if I could give him a call because he has something to tell me.

I call him.

Guess what happened:

My friend commissioned an artist to do up a book cover for him. He gives the artist a detailed description of what he wants on the cover, all the elements, etc. and lets the artist go to work. The artist does and comes back with a spitting image of what my friend wanted. Awesome, right? I know what it's like to get a book cover back from the artist and they've knocked it out of the park. There's no feeling like it and your mind starts reeling with pride, book sales projections, flashes of moments where you can show it off, etc.

So my friend is stoked and gets ready to pay the artist for the piece.

Meanwhile, the artist gets all excited about what he created and posts the book cover on Facebook. Within an hour of doing so, he contacts my friend and basically says he's not so sure my friend can have the book cover anymore.

What?

Suddenly, within that same hour, the artist turns around and tells my friend he's sold the book cover to another press. My friend is left speechless. Why would the artist do such a thing? To make matters worse, the press that acquired the cover doesn't even have a book to put it on yet, but instead decides to use it for an upcoming anthology.

The artist tells my friend that he feels super bad about it and that it's tearing him up inside, but he goes ahead and sells the piece to this press anyway.

Now my friend is left without a cover and, worse, he's just had a piece of his intellectual property stolen because the cover elements were all his concept. So he got doubly screwed.

My friend does the right thing and asks the artist if the press who acquired the image knows that it was a previously-commissioned piece. Apparently, they do. My friend goes the extra mile and writes the press and tells them very professionally what happened. The press doesn't reply.

It's sad and pathetic.

Where's the artist's integrity? Where's that press's integrity? There was absolutely no client loyalty demonstrated here. When someone hires you to do something for them, you do the job, you do it well and you hand it in. If for whatever reason you don't want to work with the person who hired you, then the task assigned to be completed falls by the wayside. It doesn't then get sold off to the next person in line. Or, in this case, people who swooped in and, in my opinion, stole the image from my friend.

This is the kind of childish and stupid behavior that is plaguing the publishing industry today, namely in the self-publishing and small press circles. It's people acting unprofessionally and screwing their peers in the business. It also goes to show the horrible state of some people's hearts and their seemingly inability to stop serving themselves.

I'm extremely disappointed in the artist and the small press who did this. I know they are people I will never work with. The thing is, word gets around. The publishing world—as big as it is—is a small world. This was a bonehead move on the part of the artist and a stupid play by the publisher.

I will add that my friend isn't one hundred percent innocent in all this. He made a single mistake in how he conducted his business: he didn't have a written contract with the artist. So let this be a lesson to you:

always have a contract, especially when working with someone you've never worked with before. It doesn't matter what it's for. If you're hiring somebody for something, get an agreement going between the two of you. It protects both parties that way.

Fortunately, my friend wasn't out any money. But he is without a cover. He's had to get someone else to draw up his concept now. Hopefully this new artist will make it even better than the last one.

In the meantime, you need to be wary of your dealings in the publishing world, whether it's with an artist, an editor, another press, even a PR person. Guard yourself. It's a cutthroat business.

36.2

I'm writing this very early in the week—Monday—so my work report this week is more so my work plan: this week I plan to make more headway on the *Fox* graphic novel and finish up the second half of the second Power Jam book. Those are the main things. If time permits, I'm going to print out the *Zomtropolis* manuscript and get it ready to transform into the *Robot City* manuscript. Again, that book is three quarters done so I want to wrap it up soon and get that out of the way before finishing *Mech Apocalypse 2.*

But, one thing at a time. For me, having multiple projects on the go can be overwhelming. Like I've said before, don't cross the streams.

36.3

2015 is a year I want to make reading a priority. I admit I've been slacking off in the novel reading department and have been focusing more on graphic novels and comics. Not that I don't consider graphic novels real books. They are, in my mind, and many are done even better than prose novels. However, I do want to get back to old-fashioned book-books. I don't have an eReader and am a paperback or hardcover guy. I like holding real books. Will I one day get into e-reading? Maybe, but I'm in no rush. I have a plethora of books on hand that need to be read so I have no need for new material anytime soon.

But reading is important because being a reader helps make you a better writer. You learn things as you read, especially if you're a writer because then your brain starts to view the story from a constructive point-of-view and not just an entertain-me point-of-view. You start to see behind the smoke and mirrors on how the sentences were constructed, see what worked and what didn't and, hopefully, end up taking those lessons into your own work.

So more reading this year. And I mean to read everything, not just fiction. It's important a writer reads everything in different styles. I have lots of non-fiction to read as well. My hope is to make a list of books I've read in 2015 and then post them on my blog when I'm done. I did this for a couple years a long time ago. It's a good habit to do and it kind of keeps me accountable to keep reading so I have something to post at the end of the year.

First thing is to finish off the couple of books I started in 2014. Then we'll move onto new stuff.

36.4

Facebook.

A social media tool that used to be a boon for writers getting the word out about their books. Every so often you'd post an "ad" for your book and you'd get a ton of views for that post thus good exposure for your work.

See, there are two types of pages on Facebook: personal and business. A writer should have both: one for their writing/book stuff, another for chatting. There can be an intermingling of the two, but typically the business page is meant for more official/professional kinds of posts, the personal page more for a here's-what-I-did-today kind of thing.

In terms of the business page, before it was great. You'd post something and get a ton of views. Now, you post something and only a very small percentage of people who liked your page see it (unless you pay Facebook to boost your post). Worse, those who see your posts are those who've elected to receive info from your page in their data stream. See, when you like a page, you choose whether to simply like it or to *also* receive updates from it.

This is where getting a lot of page likes falls through. I see writers in Facebook writers groups swapping page likes all the time—I'll like your page if you'll like mine. I've done it. It's nice to get page likes. But how many are actually selecting to receive updates from that page? You can have a million likes but if no one is receiving the actual postings, all those likes are a waste. At most, it's ego stroking. Ooh, I have a lot of people liking my page. Ooh, I must be famous.

Nonsense.

(As a side note, a quick way to get lots of likes for your page is to start a personal page, friend everyone up to the 5000 maximum, then convert that personal page into a business one. All your friends then become likes. The downside is once you convert your page, you can't post on others' timelines anymore or interact other than on your business page.)

So then you wonder what's better? Get the 5000-friend maximum on a regular Facebook page and blast out your message from there? That's great for interaction, but is it great for sales? Apparently Facebook just introduced this new thing in the New Year which basically says that posts that are blatantly ads for something get low priority in its algorithms. I've yet to test it. There might also be a penalty for constantly posting ads.

Here's the takeaway: it seems Facebook is becoming less and less of a place to sell things. It seems that Facebook wants to focus on what it was created for: socializing. So what's an author to do when they have books to sell? To not be a part of Facebook is like turning off a conduit to a major audience source.

Here's what I think the plan should be: use Facebook for socializing as it was intended. Be a person of value on there and post links to informative articles, funny videos, inspirational quotes—things of [playful] importance. Of course, be human, too, and mention that your coffee was cold this morning. In terms of pitching your books, by all means make an announcement when a new book comes out and post a purchase link. Or, I'm thinking, post a link to *where* your book can be bought. For example, instead of linking directly to Amazon, link to your book's page on your website instead, then on your website have the direct purchase links. This might be a way to bypass Facebook's "no selling" policy.

In the end, you want to fill your Facebook page with entertaining content, stuff that builds you up as an authority in your field, a cool person to know, someone people can see themselves supporting.

What about you? How has your Facebook book selling experience been?

Feel free to write in and let me know. I'm interested in your thoughts.

Speaking of thoughts, here is a collection of mine in letter form: CANADIAN SCRIBBLER: COLLECTED LETTERS OF AN UNDERGROUND WRITER. Inspiring letters that will give you a boost! http://amzn.to/1eYrNLn

End transmission.

Issue Thirty-seven - January 17, 2015

Take a look, take a see, view all that's in store for thee.

Welcome. Hope your coffee is hot.

37.1

Got the blogging machine started up again at www.canisterx.com

See, when I had my meltdown, I took down the entire site. In hindsight, I wish I hadn't, but given the circumstances at the time, it was the only choice to make. So I'm in the process of rebuilding. The website's been reloaded with book info, an interview list, a bibliography, contact info, etc. And now I'm reloading my movie reviews into it.

It's Tuesday as I write this and today I posted the eleventh review. I think I had eighty-something back in the day. Anyway, yeah, reposting those at a rate of one per day and I have enough reviews to last me the next three months. I enjoy writing the reviews and reading the reviews of others so I want to have that feature back on my website. I hope you enjoy them, too.

Will also be doing your regular blog type updates now and then when I have something to say. These will range from simply "here's what's going on" to in-depth items like articles or commentary.

I'm actually kind of glad I got rid of the old site, in a way. There was a lot of fluff on it. Not that I thought the stuff was fluff at the time of posting, but looking back, yeah, there's stuff that's gone that can stay gone. Going forward, this means that, hopefully, whatever's posted will be items of interest to those who check out the blog.

On a side note, there's an ending to that story I told last week about that artist.

Here it is:

My friend gets in touch with the artist and basically tells him he hopes that the situation was worth the artist losing X amount of dollars over. See, my friend would've used the artist more than once, so you times out the cover rate by, say, ten covers and that's a lot of dough the artist blew by acting the way he did. The artist says he never thought about it like that and regrets his decision. He then goes on to say he wants to start over with my friend, a clean slate. My friend is open to that—good on him—but the artist needs to get that original cover back in order for the fresh start to come to pass. Somehow, in the end, the artist gets the cover back and it's like the whole thing didn't happen. I guess the artist realized that whatever his reason(s) for selling the cover to that other press was wasn't worth losing a lucrative client over.

I wish both of them the best, but the lesson here is the same lesson I admonished last week: be careful when you deal with someone you're contracting work out to, especially if you've never worked with them before. Strange things happen and this little fiasco is a good example of that.

37.2

Great news on the work front. Last week I finished the first draft of the *Fox* graphic novel. It's done. I'm leaving the story alone for the next bit to let it cool down before I go back and look it over, make adjustments, add some detail, etc. It feels great the story is out on paper and out of my head. Am looking forward to checking it over when the time comes. Looking back, it's a good story and one that will make a great graphic novel once all is said and done. If you're a fan of *Sin City* and crime noir, you'll dig *Fox*.

Also on a completion note, yesterday I finished the first draft of the second Power Jam book. I'm taking today off from all fiction writing to give my brain a break then I plan to start rewrites on it tomorrow (Wednesday). My hope is to have the third draft done by the weekend/by the time you get this newsletter.

I also got the *Zomtropolis* manuscript printed out. This will be transformed into *Robot City*. Like I've said before, it's three quarters or so done. Since I'm removed from the story, I need to go over it from the beginning to get reacquainted with it. While I'm doing that, I'll also be transforming the book from a zombie apocalypse to a robot apocalypse instead. Then when that's done, it's just an issue of finishing off the tale. Since the book is done in a diary-like format, I foresee it being a fairly easy thing to wrap up quickly.

I've been also thinking about cover art for *Robot City* and a few of the elements I'd like to have on it. Soon it'll be time to get in touch with some people to help bring my vision to life.

37.3

On the reading front, I'm finishing up my 2014 book pile. I've wrapped up one book and am now finishing up the second volume of *Kane*, which is called *Rabbit Hunt*. This is written and illustrated by Paul Grist, a cartoonist I stumbled upon while reading an old issue of *Wizard* magazine a few months back. The mag reviewed *Kane* and the series caught my interest so when it was time to place an Amazon order, I added the first two volumes of *Kane* to my shopping cart.

It's a good series. It's police fiction. The art is black and white—which I love—and the stories are interesting. I think there are six volumes of *Kane* total, so I plan on getting the rest of them when the time comes.

By the time you get this newsletter, I'll be done reading this book.

37.4

Facebook group ads. Are they worth it?

Facebook is loaded with a lot of "promote your book" kinds of groups. You go in, post an ad for your book, you move on. The groups have thousands of members so on the surface these groups seem like a great way to get a ton of exposure for your work.

But do they yield sales?

My personal experience is no, they don't. What you basically have is a ton of writers all posting ads to each other about their books, but nobody's buying. Everyone just does a "drive-by spamming" and copy/pastes their ad into the group then moves onto the next one. No one really seems to be taking the time to look at the ads so, really, you're broadcasting the ads to an audience of, what, no one? Maybe a handful of people?

Seems like a waste.

While it's true some people might take interest in your book and therefore pick up a copy, my own experience with these ad groups is that they don't result in sales at all.

The argument can be made that at least you're promoting your work and exposing it to a few people. Exposure to a few people is better than none and out of those few people, if one or two buy your book, it's worth it. And I agree from that standpoint.

The question is should these book groups be viewed as viable sales channels?

Not really. While I agree one sale is better than none, it seems largely a waste of time posting to these groups just to make a couple of bucks.

On the flipside, I can see posting an ad for your free eBook as worth it. Every download you get—and you're more apt to get a download for a free book versus a paid one—will only move you further up the rankings. Then, hopefully, those who downloaded your free book will buy your other ones.

In the end, I've decided these groups aren't worth it for me anymore. I don't notice a bump in sales after posting an ad. And when I post, I post the same ad across multiple groups, which then exposes me to over ten thousand people (according to the group member numbers).

I also don't see authors I look up to posting in these groups. Instead they use Facebook to point people to their blog, inform them about a new release, and just engage with their fans.

What about you? Have you utilized these Facebook promo groups? Have you noticed an uptick in sales as a result? I'm interested in hearing your thoughts.

(And I want to thank everyone who does write in after these newsletters go out. That's part of the fun of writing them: interacting with you afterwards.)

Obligatory book ad:

First came the rain. Then came the screams. Then came the undead. BLOOD OF THE DEAD, a time travel zombie novel.
http://amzn.to/18p4VSt

End transmission.

Issue Thirty-eight - January 24, 2015

Man, time flies. Hard to believe it's been another week since one of these went out. When I was young, my dad told me that the older you get the faster time goes by. Never believed him. Of course, he was right, as he was about a lot of things.

So here we are again. Welcome.

38.1

Playing it fast and loose.

See, I recently went through a struggle with my creative work. In fact, I still struggle with it now and then, but not as much as before. Here was/is my problem: I obsess. I obsess over what I'm working on and get all worked up over making sure that what I'm writing is the best I can possibly make it. I obsess over the production aspect of turning my story into a final product for you, the reader. I obsess over the marketing of the work and I obsess over if it's a success or not.

And it's killing me.

It's killing my drive, my creativity, my emotional well-being.

Well . . . no more.

I decided over a month ago I'm going to start playing things fast and loose and have fun with this stuff again. It hasn't been an easy road to make that mental switch, but with each passing day, the choice to just "play around" with this stuff is getting easier and easier. My mood has improved, my stress levels have gone down, my head is clearer and I'm an overall better person because of it.

Ever since I started creating—circa 1994 or so—I always took it seriously and always had this urge to make something important out of whatever I was doing. This has served me well in terms of doing my best to create quality images and stories. But it's also been my downfall because it's caused all sorts of stress in my life, a lot of which came to a head last

February when I had my meltdown. Since then I've been picking up the pieces but I started going about it the wrong way. I started picking up the pieces with the mind to "make something of importance" again.

And it sucked all the fun out of it.

I've talked in this newsletter before about how magical it was writing my first book because at the time I was just writing for me and having fun with it. It was when I entered the world of publishing did things change and it became this wild goose chase of trying to make me and my books into something.

Can't do it anymore. I don't have the energy.

A couple weeks ago I called up a long-time artist friend and told him my problem. I basically told him all I've just told you. In the end, he related a story about something he used to work on—an old project—and how "turning it into something" ended up harming the work and his relationship with the writer of the comic. Last year, him and his writer friend started talking again and got around to discussing resurrecting this comic strip of theirs. And this is when my friend said something that stuck out to me. He said they'd do the strip without any expectations. They'd do it without trying to make it into a big deal, without trying to make it well known, and just do it for the fun of it.

That resonated with me and was something I needed to hear. It's easy to get all caught up with creating for success and taking the projects too seriously. I don't want to be in that place anymore.

I'm not saying I'm going to stop caring or that I'm going to turn out just whatever or even that I've lost ambition. What I am saying is I'm making the conscious choice to just play around with my art and writing and do it without expectation. Just do it because I'm an artist and creating is what I do. It's what I *need* to do.

As said, changing my perspective has made things a lot easier. I'm actually starting to have fun again and that, my friends, is a success all its own.

38.2

It's Wednesday as I do this write up. The second Power Jam book went to the artist yesterday, so between that and the first one, he'll be busy for next while getting the images together. This frees up my headspace to focus on other things as I'm going to lay the Power Jam stories down for a while and wait until these first two books are published before writing up some more. I have plans for ten books in this series so here's hoping for more to be created before the year is out.

My next item on the to-do list is to do the second draft of the *Fox* graphic novel. This is straight forward. This is just me reading what I wrote and making a few tweaks and/or adding some expansion to the panel descriptions. After this stage is done, then the book will be ready to go into the art stage of character design.

Doing the *Fox* rewrite should take me to the end of the week. It'll be on the weekend or Monday I'll start up transforming *Zomtropolis* into *Robot City*. I've been thinking about the storyline and how I'm going to make the change of turning it from a horror into a sci-fi. I have some ideas. After I work through the manuscript, then I'll finish it up.

I also started talking to an artist about the cover, so it's coming together.

38.3

Been reading *The Imagination Manifesto* by GMB Chomichuck et al. GMB was the artist who did the cover to *Mech Apocalypse*. I'm on graphic novel two of three in the series. Each book contains five serialized graphic novels so you get a portion of each story with each *Imagination Manifesto*. It's a surreal read with interesting concepts, writing styles and artwork. I'm particularly fond of *The Tomorrow Society*, which is a superhero tale. (Go figure.)

GMB's got a few other graphic novels out there so I plan to get my hands on those soon after finishing *The Imagination Manifesto* books.

38.4

With social media losing its appeal/ability for direct advertising, writers and artists need to look at other ways to promote their work.

The secret is having a core audience of people who are genuinely interested in what you do and, in turn, are willing to spend money on the stuff you create. But where do you find them? How do you get their attention?

One of the ways is to start a newsletter like this one. A newsletter is a way to get access to people who've *chosen* to receive information from you. For me, this is a godsend because I'm interested in genuine readers and fans, not just a bunch of "empty" social media connections.

So start a newsletter as a way to connect with your audience and a way to market to them directly.

Make your newsletter about something. As a newsletter reader myself, I enjoy when the writer of it puts in actual content instead of just a bunch of ads for their books. I'm interested in what's going on in that creator's life, what they're working on, their thoughts on various issues. I'm not interested in just receiving notices about new releases. I think that in this day and age, it's important for creators to open up and form relationships with readers instead of just marketing to them cold. Sure, you can get away with this if you're a big name already. Some people just want to hear about when Joe Famous has a new book coming out. But for those of us who are still building our audience, creating a connecting point with our readers is important. This where newsletters like this one and blogging comes in. I don't know about you, but I'm more apt to buy something from someone I know versus someone I don't.

So you have your newsletter idea. The next step is to decide on how you're going to send it out. There are many options out there, everything from sending it out via your own email to a bunch of BCC's, to using an email service like MailChimp or TinyLetter. I use the latter. It's free, simple and does a good job for a text-based newsletter like this one.

Once you have your newsletter and emailing platform selected—and have also decided how often you're going to send it out—the next step is to tell everyone about it.

Post your newsletter link everywhere via your blog, Twitter, Facebook,

Google+, LinkedIn, email signature line—everywhere. Add it to your business cards. Have a signup sheet at book signings so you can capture email addresses. If you want, you can even sweeten the pie by offering something free to those who sign up, whether this is a free short story or even novel. eBook, of course.

I have mixed feelings on using the freebie bribe because then I wonder if people signed up solely for the freebie or because they were genuinely interested in me. At the same time, if indeed they signed up only for the freebie, at least they're signed up and then your job is to convert them via your newsletter into actual fans. I've yet to experiment with this.

This just an overview of starting up a newsletter. I'm sure we'll talk more about using a newsletter to build up your reader base in the future.

Commercial:

Angels. Demons. Giant zombies. A war is raging. POSSESSION OF THE DEAD, a time travel zombie thriller. http://amzn.to/1fvlf7g

End transmission.

Issue Thirty-nine - January 31, 2015

Welcome back. I hope everybody had a good week. Mine was not too bad. Had some highs, had some lows. Still fighting.

39.1

Fragments . . .

Had a business meeting with a studio this past week to go over some items. In the end, it was decided that I'd write for them an original graphic novel based on an idea between myself and the studio. So far the basic premise has been decided upon and a general "here's what's going to go down." Look forward to starting it once I finish up a couple other projects.

. . .

Got behind on the work front as I had a medical procedure last Friday and then my mom came for a visit on the weekend. No matter. Family's more important than any of this stuff anyway. Was good to spend time with her as I love having her around.

. . .

Been struggling with sleep issues. Not lack of sleep, but too much sleep. Seems like I can't get enough and am averaging around twelve hours a day. All that down time certainly makes for some interesting dreams, but I'm coming to a place where I think I'm going to have to pull back on the sack-time hours and cut it to eight or nine. Too much sleep makes you tired.

. . .

Been soaking up a lot of comic book inspiration by way of following many comic creators on Twitter. I love seeing their works-in-progress, thoughts on the industry, drawing tips and just whatever's on their mind. Helps spur me on in my own endeavours.

. . .

Further to the above, I bounce back and forth between wanting to take a break from writing books and just getting into comics for a while. It seems book writing isn't a sustainable way to make a living anymore, with the market being flooded, and I'm wondering if there's more room for new voices in the comic book field. It was comics, after all, that got me started on my creative journey. Not sure. Still noodling with this idea.

39.2

The second draft of the *Fox* graphic novel is complete. The edits that I kept making to it were forgotten question marks. When I write longhand—as this script had been done—I write really fast to keep the momentum going so it makes sense I'd discover some punctuation errors on the second read through.

As mentioned, I met with a studio this week so that's another project to add to the to-do list. Right now the project is in the idea phase so I'm going to let it just percolate in the brain for the time being and let it coalesce into its own thing before committing anything to paper.

It's Thursday as I write this and I still haven't started redrafting *Zomtropolis*. Perhaps I'll start tonight. Today's writing goal is to do this newsletter. Speaking of which, we have thirteen issues to go after this one and then Year One of the newsletter will be complete, which means I'll be collecting the first year of issues into a book. That'll come out June-ish. Though you've gotten this newsletter free, might be nice to have a hardcopy for the archives. I'm thinking of prefacing the collected edition with a newsletter exclusive to that edition.

39.3

This past week saw the release of the trailer for the *Fantastic Four* reboot. You can watch it here:
https://www.youtube.com/watch?v=cxIldZcUuCk

It looks like quite the sci-fi movie and seems to want to attempt to do something new with the Fantastic Four premise. I think the director came out and said he was really going for a hard sci-fi flick with this thing as opposed to a superhero movie. Which, for me, is sad because if you're going to adapt a superhero comic book into a movie, it should be a superhero movie in the end. I'm all for trying new things so I could very well be proven wrong once this movie comes out, but I would have liked it to retain some form of superhero vibe as opposed to a sci-fi flick. Personally, I liked the previous Fantastic Four movies. Were they perfect? No. Were they fun? Yes. Were they *superhero* movies? Yup.

We'll chalk this up to the "we'll see" category for now.

39.4

Last week I suggested you start a newsletter to connect with your readers. For me, I love the newsletter format. It's like being able to write a letter to you guys every week, ask how's it going and be able to tell you a little bit about what's going on with me, both personally and creatively.

So if you start a newsletter, you need to decide on the content.

There's a million and one things you can do. I took a cue for my own newsletter from Warren Ellis's *Oribital Operations* in terms of getting personal with you guys. I then added my own "selling feature" by including a publishing and marketing tip in each issue because I want to connect with other creative people. The fandom stuff I mention is to appeal to the comic fans on my list as well as give me a chance to talk about superheroes, which are a big part of my life. I then end off every newsletter with a book ad to let you guys know about one of my stories in the hopes that you will check it out.

For your own newsletter, you can do what I do or do something of your own. I do suggest including personal tidbits in it as that makes you human and brings you down to earth instead of being one of those "untouchable" authors.

I also most definitely suggest including some sort of promo aspect to it because part of the purpose of a newslist is to create an audience you can market to.

Some writers just do promo-only newsletters and you get one every time they have a new release. This works fine if a) the author doesn't have the inclination or time to commit to a regular newsletter and b) that author is famous anyway and people simply want to know when that author has a new book out.

I like Piers Anthony's newsletter, which you can read on his website (www.hipiers.com) This one is a monthly newsletter that he's had going for a long time in which he talks about what he's working on, books he's read, movies he's watched, some thoughts on various issues. Sort of a giant blog cramming what could have been several separate blog entries into one. It's easy maintenance for him because he only has to post once a month and call it good.

Offering behind-the-scenes info on your creative process is also good. September17 Production's newsletter (http://eepurl.com/bcL6Dv) does this and you get glimpses into what's going on in their comic book production prior to any of the comics being released. As an author, you can share snippets of works-in-progress or even an entire chapter, if you want to.

You can also provide a balance of the two, which Christine Steendam does with her newsletter. (You also get a free eBook when you sign up for hers.) It's at http://eepurl.com/UKdW9

In the end, you need to decide what information you're going to convey to the reader. You should also ask yourself why they would even bother signing up to begin with, that is, are you providing something of value or are you just going to talk about your books and/or just make each issue one giant ad?

Another option is to serialize a novel and send it out via email, one chapter every week or something. Put a promo at the end where folks can buy the book in its entirety and/or include links to your other work.

Please also note, too, you don't have to follow the above examples. If there's something you want to see in a newsletter and no one's doing it, why don't you do it? Would certainly make you stand out from the crowd.

The possibilities are endless. You can do your newsletter weekly, bi-weekly, monthly, every six months—up to you. I just think having one's an important tool in the writer's promotional toolbox.

If you're stuck for ideas, consider signing up for a handful of author newsletters and see what they're doing and draw inspiration from those.

And if you do start a newsletter, email me and let me know so I can sign up for it.

To end off:

Zombies. The devil. War. A wild adventure through a post-apocalyptic world. REDEMPTION OF THE DEAD. http://amzn.to/1rFWKWm

End transmission.

Issue Forty - February 7, 2015

Roses are red
Violets are blue
Words are sweet
This newsletter's for you

Or something.

sigh

40.1

Fragments . . .

I've written about the stresses this business can bring upon a creator and how sometimes the fun gets sucked out of it. I'm pleased to report this week was a good week. It wasn't hugely productive but in terms of my headspace and inner feelings toward the biz, I'm coming around to a place of finally relaxing again and having the urge to just play around. To me, this signifies a breakthrough in writing from the heart versus just writing from the head. The former is where quality comes from because, like cooking, you can tell if love has been put into a creative piece or not. I want my books and comics to be read with a sense of heart behind the stories and not just superficial entertainment.

. . .

Journaling. I consider myself a loose journaler. I don't have private diaries or anything like that because my writing has always been a way for me to work out my issues/reflect on various situations. I also blog about what's going on and I have this newsletter, which is a kind of journal. However, our church is doing a study on the book of Mark with an assignment of reading one chapter per week. The aim is to read that chapter three times throughout the course of the week and journal your thoughts on it each time (i.e. lessons learned, questions raised, reflect on the real life application of what you just read, etc.). I'm finding it a challenge. I can be contemplative over what I read, but articulating my thoughts on the page is a bit tougher. I know, I know. A writer struggling with writing. Go figure. At the same time, not only is this a good spiritual discipline but it's also a good writing exercise because it forces my brain to think in a different way than I'm used to and to write out my thoughts directly verses veiling them in fiction. Good practice.

Are any of you journalers?

. . .

Thinking of Facebook and how it's becoming a useless marketing tool for the writer. I have two pages. One is my author page (http://www.facebook.com/apfuchsbooks) and the other is my personal page (www.facebook.com/apfuchs) The former is promo only and nothing personal, the latter is where I socialize and do some promo. The organic reach isn't the same as the old days and, it seems, fewer and fewer people are seeing the posts. Sure, I can pay to boost them, but that's not in the budget.

Wondering what the next big social media splash is going to be and how it can be used to get my books in front of people.

. . .

So far I only have one planned appearance this year and that's at the Central Canada Comic Con in the fall. I did smaller shows last year but with the table fees for those shows having tripled this year, tabling has become too expensive for those events in terms of Return on Investment. I hope my local comic shop does an artist showcase again for Free Comic Book Day. It was a huge success for me last year.

Might do a couple signings throughout the year to help boost awareness of me and my books.

. . .

Thinking on how many of you read this newsletter. I can see my open rates via the stats page at TinyLetter, but I also promote this newsletter when it posts via social media channels. Don't know how to see a hit count for those. Just something that's going through my mind today (Friday).

40.2

I really liked my original title for *Robot City*, which was *Zomtropolis.* The "tropolis" part is very appealing and conveys what the story is about. Unfortunately, there's a *Robotropolis* movie out there (a fun B-flick, which I've seen), so the title's taken and though titles aren't copyrighted, I try to come up with original titles for my work. Am thinking of maybe rebranding the book as *Robtropolis.* It's similar, but different. I don't know. We'll see.

The edits on switching the book from a zombie story to a killer robot one are started.

In a holding pattern regarding the *Power Jam* books. Both of them are with the artist so my part is done for now. All I can do is wait until the drawings for each are completed before I can move onto the next phase.

40.3

In fanboy news, nothing huge has come down the wire this week. At least, nothing that I think is worth noting here. There's always comic and superhero movie news, but no headline really scratched my itch.

So I'll do this section differently and talk about art this week. My art.

I can draw comics. I'm not the greatest artist in the world, but I don't downright suck either. Been wanting to get back into producing artwork regularly again. It'll be an opportunity to hone my skills, improve weaknesses, and be another way to exercise that creative part of my brain.

I laid awake last night thinking about it and really found myself wanting to not only get regular with my line art again, but also teach myself to color that artwork. I can do basic coloring in terms of red goes here, green goes there, but to do what's called modeling in the comic book field, I don't know how to do that. Will have to do some reading and study on it. Youtube videos will be a way to learn how to color digitally as well. This can open doors for freelance work for me.

40.4

This week's publishing tip is a writing one and this particular tip applies to the artist as well.

Here it is: don't overthink it.

There are times when writing a story where you seem to hit a brick wall. I'm not talking about writer's block, but there are moments now and then where you really have to grind the gears to get an idea out on paper. Could be a complicated plot point, could be a sequence of dialogue, could be a continuity thing. Sometimes I find myself mulling over what needs to come next in the story and thinking about it too hard. This then usually leads to a bout of anxiety, a sore head and a frustrated heart.

The thing is, the human brain is a remarkable machine which operates not just on a conscious platform, but a subconscious one as well. This why you're able to keep track of a story from points A to Z without consciously thinking about every point in between.

My advice if you're hung up on a scene is to stop thinking about it and just let the idea(s) come instead of mining your brain for something to write. Trust your instincts. Just let it flow. If you're at a point where the story has come to a stop, mentally go over what you wrote (i.e. this happened then this happened, etc.) and then let the next logical progression come to you naturally instead of ransacking your brain and forcing the issue. It might be a grand idea, it might be a simple one. Either way, that's your jumping off point to keep going.

Same with drawing. You can get hung up on a detail to your piece (i.e. you can't draw a hand for the life of you), so put the pencil down and walk away. Instead of forcing the image of what it's supposed to look like in your mind's eye, *casually* or *superficially* think about it instead, then get back to the drawing board and let your hand take over instead of your brain.

Overthinking your art can lead to making it into more of a big deal than it is and cause a break in creative output. Instead, just let your brain do its thing and let your imagination come up with whatever it comes up—like a runaway thought—and put that down instead.

I'm not talking about writing nonsense. I'm talking about putting your conscious and analytical thinking in the backseat and letting your brain follow its thought patterns without hindrance.

Most writers will tell you of experiences where they've lost themselves in their story, where they've been typing and the next thing they know an hour has passed. I've had moments like that where I'm *living* what I'm writing, like a dream, and when I do snap out of it, it's a bit jarring. That kind of head flow is what I'm talking about here. In those deep writing moments, I wasn't *thinking*, I was just *doing*, was just following the rabbit trail.

Your brain's already got it figured out. The issue is if you're going to receive that final package of story or not.

Overthinking is like putting a No Mail sign up for the delivery guy.

Capisce?

End transmission.

Issue Forty-one - February 14, 2015

Happy Romance Day, everyone. Whether you're spending this holiday with someone or alone, at least know that this writer is sending out his love to you.

Thanks for reading.

41.1

Deadlines have been on my mind this week, both personal ones and the concept in general. Deadlines are a good thing in that they ensure that things get done. To have things completely open-ended can lead to unproductivity. At the same time, having too many deadlines or ones without enough lead time can also be as detrimental.

As an independent publisher and writer, I have the luxury of not having any deadlines. There's no one breathing down my neck to get something done by a certain date. This is incredibly freeing because it takes the pressure off having to *immediately* produce something. However, if I don't maintain some form of discipline in my creative habits, then I run the risk of not doing anything at all.

In the back of my mind, I have one master deadline and that's the big comic show in the fall. I table there every year and I want to make sure I have, at minimum, one new offering for the show. From a personal accomplishment standpoint, I'm fine with that, just having the one new project.

But what about all the other projects I have on the go? When should those come out? This is where pacing oneself and experience comes in. I know roughly how long it'll take me to finish something and I know roughly how long it'll take to get that project through production and out to the public, so I kind of block in X amount of time for each task and ballpark when the book is going to be out. I then further breakdown those blocks of time into manageable chunks so I get a certain amount of work done each week to ensure I get the project completed within a certain timeframe. This way I'm not buckling under pressure and am not sitting down every day forcing myself to write something. I can simply pace myself and let the story come out naturally instead.

The flip side is, in theory, the more consistently you put out books, the more money you'll make because you're always feeding your readers something new. But, as said, this is in theory because the market's so flooded right now that unless you have a sizable following, frequency isn't that much of a factor.

In the end, I'm just grateful that I have a loose plan for when stuff is going to come out. If I hit those deadlines, great. If I don't, no big deal as long as I have at least one new thing for comic con in the fall.

That's where I'm at these days in terms of deadlines and how I feel about them. It's an ongoing thing and is always subject to change.

41.2

Good news and bad news on the *Zomtropolis* front, so here's the bad news first: I tried going through the book to see if it was possible to switch it from a zombie novel into a killer robot one. I thought the task would be simple, as in just switching out the monsters for robots, maybe a couple other tweaks and that's it. Turns out this wasn't the case and the book is specifically written as a zombie apocalypse, everything from the descriptions to the action sequences, to the commentary of what it's like living in a post-apocalyptic world. So, in short, my plans to turn it into a sci-fi fell through and I'm going to have to finish it as a monster book. It's either that or rewrite the whole book, which I'm not prepared to do.

The good news: the book is extremely well-written and carries a lot of depth and meaning within its pages. It's very emotional and very heavy, but in a good way. Aside from doing a round of edits on the material I have, I was also able to outline the ending so now have that broken down scene-by-scene. All I need to do now is expand on those scenes to finish the book.

As a side note, something weird happened after I finished the round of edits. All the ideas I had to finish the book were coming at me at once in a hodge podge of mental chaos, so much so my head hurt and I was getting terribly confused. To combat this, I let the ideas stew in my head for a couple days then sat down and pulled the ideas one by one out of the fray and untangled the mess. Now I have my outline for the rest of the book. This is a first for me since I never outline. Normally a story comes to me in a linear fashion: this happens then this happens then this happens, etc. Not so with this one. It'll be an interesting experience to work off an outline for a novel. I have a bit of experience in that the *Fox* graphic novel was written off of an outline so I'm familiar with looking at notes for a scene then expanding it.

At least from a creative heavy lifting perspective, that aspect is done because I already mapped out the key events until the end therefore don't have to think of them anymore.

41.3

Read *Rizzo: Year One* this week. It's by Chris Riseley and Sean Simmans. It's a comic strip series that started around 2005, ran for a few years, faded away, then has recently come back. I'm a huge Sean Simmans fan and he's one of my favorite cartoonists. Had the pleasure of working with him in the past and he's always been a good source of artistic wisdom when I've needed it.

Rizzo follows the exploits of Cragen Tiberious Rizzowski, his friend Bill—who was a mascot for the Tromso Reptiles and has yet to take off his lizard suit—Rizzo's wife Roberta, and a supporting cast like Byron, Andy, Delroy and others.

The strips are everything from poking fun at everyday life, to bashing the political powers that be, to commentary on marriage, and, given Rizzo's and Bill's jobs, trying to eke out a living as cartoonists. (You see, Bill and Rizzo do the comic strip *Rizzo,* which is based on their exploits.)

What's cool about this series is though the strips are usually three-panel gags, there's an actual storyline that runs through all of them, with some strips referencing the other strips that came before. It's not just a series of one-off jokes and that's it. Each strip is part of a cohesive whole.

I have the first book collecting the *Rizzo* strips and rumor has it a second one is on its way. I, for one, am eager to get my hands on it when the time comes.

For more on *Rizzo*, check it out on-line at
www.facebook.com/rizzocomics

and

www.rizzodaily.com

41.4

I'm part of a writer's group online and new authors keep asking about the need for ISBNs (International Standard Book Number). The main question that keeps popping up is, are they needed?

The answer is yes. They are needed. They are how the book industry keeps track of book titles. Each ISBN is an identifier of a certain book.

If you have a publisher, then you don't need to worry about them. They'll take care of obtaining an ISBN number(s) for you. That's their job.

If you are publishing independently, you will need to obtain an ISBN number(s) yourself.

There are a few ways to do this.

The easy way is to obtain one through places like Createspace or Smashwords if you're publishing through them. You will need one ISBN per format of your book, so if you're publishing in paperback *and* eBook, you'll need an ISBN for each. By getting these ISBNs, it'll enable your book to be available for sale through the various retail channels these publishing platforms have access to.

If you've read my how-to book on self-publishing, *Getting Down and Digital: How to Self-publish Your Book*, you know I advocate starting up your own press via your own company. There are lots of reasons to do this. See the book for more info.

Once your company is established, you'll need to obtain ISBNs for the book(s) you're going to put out. These can be obtained through various sources, depending on where you live. Likewise, where you live will determine if there is a fee to obtaining one.

In Canada, go to this website to get your free ISBNs:

www.collectionscanada.gc.ca/ciss-ssci/index-e.html

In the US, go to:

www.isbn.org/standards/home/index.asp

In the UK, go to:

www.isbn.nielsenbook.co.uk/controller.php?page=158

In Australia, go to:

www.myidentifiers.com.au

For all other countries, Google "Where to get ISBNs in (country name)" and follow the appropriate results.

One of the pluses of having your own publishing imprint and corresponding ISBNs is part of the ISBN number identifies your company as the publisher of the book, making it your own.

Once you have your ISBNs, you can use these when asked for the information when setting up your title with different distribution channels. As said, these distribution channels require books to have an ISBN in order to keep track of things.

Hope the above clears things up.

Zombies, werewolves, vampires, robots and more all duke it out in Bloodsport-like battles in ZOMBIE FIGHT NIGHT.
http://amzn.to/19NgUrj

End transmission.

Issue Forty-two - February 21, 2015

Can't believe it's been another week. This past one was a weird one for me and I was dealing with a few things. Still recovering, but am doing better. Besides, I've had a runny nose for two weeks and it's still not letting up. You should see my tissue bill.

42.1

Writing and creating is a funny job. Out of all the jobs in the world, it's one of the few that, it seems, you're on-call for 24/7. The brain never lets up and round the clock you're getting ideas upon ideas for future stories or things on the writing/production to-do list. For years, I worked what you could consider sixteen-hour days, stopping only to sleep. Not that I was writing for sixteen hours straight every day, but I'd be working on my own stuff or editing someone's book or formatting that book or drawing . . . and it'd last all day. I'd stop for supper and lunch, my coffee breaks or to spend time with family, but mentally I was always working and picking at things when I had a spare moment. I've been pretty much working/creating that way since 2000.

I think it's caught up to me. I'm feeling worn out and have had enough in a lot of ways. I know people typically slow down when they get older. Maybe that's what's happening to me. It's been a good long while since I've worked round the clock on this stuff. That, and I'm in a place where I'm learning balance and knowing when to cut things off for the day. That's not to say I'm giving up on any of this or anything. Just saying I'm making time for other things like spending time with my family (which I didn't do a lot of before). I'm finding around the evening is when I'll shut things down for the day and whatever didn't get done that day will go on tomorrow's docket. It's been incredibly restful for the body and for the mind. I don't feel like I have a thousand voices going off in my head anymore.

The point of all this is I think balance needs to be part of every creator's life. They need to know when to be all gung ho and go hard, and also when to pull on the reins and slow down. Like the saying goes, you can't run a racehorse every day.

How are you balancing things?

42.2

So this week writing has taken a back seat for several reasons, but the main one is I'm behind on a freelance gig I told someone I was going to do. It's a book layout project involving lots of scanning and repositioning images on a page. And since it's paying work, I've got to give it priority over my other stuff. I want to do a good job on this so am keeping this project at the fore of my mind for now.

42.3

This week was a reading blitz of Alec Longstreth comics. Alec, who's a super nice guy, does a minicomic called *Phase 7*. He's been doing it for years and has released twenty-one issues so far. I have a couple trade paperbacks collecting some of these issues as well as all five *Phase 7* issues containing his five-part story/graphic novel, *Basewood*.

Alec is a gifted cartoonist and the guy lives and breathes comics. His stuff is also mostly autobiographical stories and I see a lot of myself in them. Always good to read something relatable.

I needed a pick-me-up this past week and I found Alec's comics made me feel better.

For more, go to his website at www.alec-longstreth.com

42.4

On February 12th I attended Christine Steendam's book launch at McNally Robinson's. She launched three books. Yes, three. Pretty impressive. It was a cool format in that she had CBC radio's Terry MacLeod do a live interview with her. Never seen that format before, but her launch is what inspired this week's marketing tip. You guessed it: book launches.

A book launch is different than a book signing. For your regular run-of-the-mill signing, you basically show up, sign books, go home. A book launch is more a celebration of a new release. It's a party. It's a "launch" and not a mere signing.

I did one for my novel *The Way of the Fog* way back in 2005 and made it an event. Aside from inviting everyone I knew, I made up mini brochures to hand out to everyone promoting the book. There was a reading, a Q&A, a signing and drinks and cookies. I'm pretty sure I served coffee as well. It was great because after the more formal part of the launch (i.e. the reading and Q&A), I signed books and got to talk to people about the novel. I also got to socialize over some tasty treats.

Christine's launch was similar in that after she had done the live interview, she did a draw for a prize basket, signed some books, and served up wine, super fancy baking, and had this cake which was a replica of one of her books.

The point is, her and my launches were events. We crafted a party around the release of a new title. This is good because not only is it fun for those you've invited, it's also something that catches the interest of other people in the store. They see a book launch going on and often come over and sneak a seat to see what the book and author are all about. This leads to more sales and getting more readers on board for your work.

Likewise, you can also send out a press release about it and invite the media to attend. This is a great chance to get your book featured on the radio, TV, newspaper or Internet.

Book launches can also be a tool for networking as you never know who's in the audience. My friend Andrew Lorenz was at Christine's launch and he ended up talking to Terry MacLeod after. Andrew then introduced me to Terry and guess what? He and I are going to be on CBC radio this coming Sunday a little after 8 AM to talk about comic books and working in the superhero genre. Tune in, if you get a chance. (I think http://www.cbc.ca/weekendmorning/ will work.)

As a warning, book launches can be expensive because it's up to you or potentially your publisher to provide all the extras like food and drinks for your launch party. However, there are cost-effective ways of doing this (i.e. home baking, bringing a giant urn of coffee, etc.).

In the end, having a party about your book gets people excited about it and hopefully they'll tell others about you and your work once the launch is over.

A book launch is something every author should do at least once in their career so contact your local store and ask about setting one up.

Speaking of books:

Like superheroes? Like zombies? Then you'll love METAHUMANS vs the UNDEAD. It's Ultimate Good vs Ultimate Evil!
http://amzn.to/1dIbc81

End transmission.

Issue Forty-three - February 28, 2015

Welcome to the forty-third issue of *The Canister X Transmission.* So far I've been able to send this newsletter out weekly without missing a beat.

Forty-three weeks and counting.

Not bad.

Back issues can be read at www.tinyletter.com/apfuchs This is also the link you can share with other folks if you think they'd like/benefit from this newsletter. Thanks.

43.1

Been learning how to pace myself lately. I'm coming out of a season of internal chaos, where my thoughts and feelings were all over the map, where anxiety complete with breathing trouble was the norm, and the inability to settle down was routine.

That's being transparent.

What I'm learning out of all of this—amongst other things—is how to compartmentalize my thoughts and feelings into boxes which I can set aside and then address one at a time. Instead of dealing with a giant chaotic mess all in one shot, I can go through things and accomplish tasks one at a time instead. The byproduct of this is not only are things slowly getting done, but I'm not an anxiety-ridden maniac when doing them.

This "compartmentalization" is also helping me when I mentally look at all the upcoming projects I have. You've seen the previous newsletters where I've discussed my current book commitments and what I have planned for the future. Sometimes being creative can be exhausting because the ideas keep coming and you keep wanting to start different projects—and you do—and then one day you're so far down the rabbit hole you don't know who you are anymore. Now I'm able to tackle what I need to do one thing at a time and with each crossing of an item off the list, the lighter I feel and the easier things seem.

Don't know if you're in the same boat with your own projects, but my advice would be to step back, take a breath, and then work through each item one at a time. They'll get done and you'll feel better afterward.

43.2

Been enjoying doing this layout project for an acquaintance. It's not writing, but it is creative and a chance to stretch my graphic design muscles. That's what I've been working on since last newsletter. Probably have about another week to go until the project is all scanned in and ready for first-draft presentation. Then it'll just be an issue of possibly making a few minor adjustments before the file is ready for print. This is also giving my brain a rest from writing and having to make stuff up. Again, this goes back to my newfound love for compartmentalization and working through items—big and small—one at a time.

More productive this way.

After this freelance gig, it'll be time to finish *Zomtropolis,* which is already outlined. Just needs fleshing out.

43.3

I'm a huge indie comics fan, a combination of my love for comic books and the do-it-yourself tenacity and perseverance that independent publications require.

This past week I've been on a Julia Wertz binge and read through all three of her books that I have in my collection: *The Fart Party*, *The Fart Party* Vol. 2, and *Drinking at the Movies.* Don't let the titles fool you. There are only a couple of fart jokes in the books and no real parties. There is drinking at the movies, though. They're autobiographical tales from Julia's life, all told in short segments and/or gags, all collected between two covers.

Julia's one of the cartoonists I admire thanks to her sharp wit, concise storytelling ability and her just plain honesty in her work. If she's having a good day, she'll tell you why. If she's having a bad day and everything she touches turns to crap, you'll know about it, too. No pretension on her part. She's tells you about her life as it is, the good, the bad and the ugly.

I find this stuff encouraging, especially where I'm at these days with a few areas of my life being down in the dumps. To know there are others out there duking out this battle that we call the human existence, well, it spurs me on to keep fighting the good fight.

Thanks, Julia.

For more on Julia Wertz and her comics, please visit www.juliawertz.com

I know I'm due for a visit there since she has another book out that I don't have and that I want for my collection.

43.4

This segment is inspired by something I've done in the past and was recently confirmed while reading through one of Alec Longstreth's *Phase 7* collections.

Trading.

This is a method of self-promotion I seldom—if ever—see talked about when people talk about marketing their books or comics.

Sure, it's not a money-maker—though it could be from an awareness/long term point-of-view—but it's a means to get your name out there and get some new books and comics out of it in return.

Conventions or through the mail would be the way to go about doing this, and I've traded my books for books and comics of others. Instead of them buying from me or me buying from them, we just swapped titles. And we both won because I was able to expose someone new to my work that might not have spent any money on me, and I got a new book/comic to read as well, in turn exposing me to someone new. Who knows? They like your stuff, they'll tell others. It also gets copies of your work circulating the convention floor instead of having stacks of your stuff on your table.

Trading doesn't have to be a "dollar for dollar" deal either in terms of value. I mean, though you might charge $15 for your book even though it only cost you $4 to print, you don't need to exchange it for $15 in books or comics. You could just swap it for $4 in comics or a book that cost only $3 for someone else to print. You don't need to penny pinch about it.

Vendors also sell other things at conventions besides book and comics, so if there's that trinket you wanted or action figure that's caught your eye, see if the vendor will be willing to trade for it.

Trading is also a great way to network because it forces you to talk to other creators, share publication stories, printing tips, creative processes, compare books, etc.

And if the other guy doesn't want to trade? No big deal. You can be nice and leave a copy of your work anyway or just move on to the next table.

Again, I realize you can't pay the bills with trades, but if you're able to gain a few lifetime fans with them, it's worth it because when your next project comes out, they'll either spend money on you or swap with you for another of your own.

And if you're addicted to books and comics like I am, trading is a good way to get "free" stuff and keep the reading/entertainment train going.

Don't forget to trade autographs, too!

Here's an ad. This one's to buy a book, not trade. Reading is good for you.

End transmission.

Issue Forty-four - March 7, 2015

Welcome to Saturday. Another week down. Some weeks take their sweet time to go by and others just whiz right past. I'm not a fan of either extreme. A happy middle ground would be nice. I could live there.

Here's *The Canister X Transmission* number forty-four.

44.1

Alan Moore, the famed comics writer, once said something profound. He said, "All stories are true." Was thinking about that statement this past week and upon reflection, I have to agree with him.

Here's my reasoning:

While it's clearly impossible for any story presented as it is to be true (i.e. Superman turning back time to save Lois Lane), it is a true statement that *truth* is woven into all fiction, whether we're talking books, comics, movies, whatever.

There's an old writer's adage to "write what you know." In truth, writing what one knows is all any writer can write. If you don't know something, you can't write about it. You don't know what you don't know, you know? That said, it stands to reason that all stories carry within their pages elements of truth from a writer's life. They can be very blatant truths as in here's a situation the writer went through in reality and therefore they're going to write about it, to basing characters off of real people, to crafting a story which states the writer's view on a particular topic, to even going so far as a story being a writer's fantasy about a particular area.

Looking back on my own work, there is much truth and real life woven into the stories as there is fiction. Even how my characters react to a certain situation is an extension of how I would react to that situation if I was in their shoes (and, while writing those scenes, I *am* in their shoes). Situations my characters deal with, their pasts, their ups and downs, are all based on portions of reality as I've experienced it through the years. I write what I know and put a piece(s) of me into my stories.

If you were to pull apart my work and separate the elements within it that are based on real life experiences and then hold those experiences up against my life story as it's been thus far, you'd see the crossovers quite clearly.

Therefore, my stories are true.

And if my stories are true, then so are other creators' stories that find their way onto paper.

Granted, we're not talking *pure* truth. We're talking elements of truth.

I think by recognizing this fact, it adds a whole new dimension to whatever story you happen to be reading at the moment. To understand that the writer has put doses of their reality—what they understand to be true—in their fiction, elevates the work to a whole new level. It also makes a kind of fun guessing game out of the whole thing as you try and figure out what might be true about a tale and what's just filler.

Something to consider as you read this week.

44.2

It's Thursday as I write this. Still working on that layout project. I haven't been working eight hours a day on it, more just here and there. I'm about halfway done. I'm finding it simple work, nice and relaxing. It's also getting me back into being comfortable working with Photoshop since the last time I really used the program for layout was when I put together the *Mech Apocalypse* cover.

Also talked with the artist to the *Power Jam* books the other day. Was told he's going to scan and send me some stuff soon. Look forward to seeing what he's come up with based on my descriptions outlined in the narrative.

Then I got this newsletter and I do count the writing of it as part of my creative output. It is going to be collected in a book, after all, and will be part of my overall body of work that folks can look back on after I die. This newsletter has been a godsend for me in terms of being a place I can empty my mind on a few issues week to week, instead of having these thoughts circulate and take up headspace and clutter up the mental works.

Onward.

44.3

After having gone through a recent bout of prolonged anxiety, I've developed a kind of hibernation routine that has become a sanctuary for me both mentally and physically.

Very simply: comics/graphic novels in bed.

I've been nestling in whenever I get a chance and just go under the covers and read. Lately, autobio comics have been my drug of choice as I tend to relate to a lot of what's going on in those stories. Again, sharing the human experience with another—even if it's through drawn panels—has brought a great sense of comfort to me because often when we're going through crisis, we feel like we're the only ones in the world experiencing the hardships of being a human being. If that's you reading this, know you're not alone. We all got crap we're dealing with. Sometimes it comes in waves, sometimes in little bumps.

Been reading *Alec: The Years Have Pants* by Eddie Campbell this week. It's a giant, 600-plus-page tome collecting all of Eddie's autobiographical *Alec* books plus extra material. I'm only a page 44 as I type this up. The books within the book go over his history as a factory worker, to being a full time artist, to being married and having kids, to people he's known over the years. It's definitely a series of stories about simply living life as he's filtered them through his autobiographical counterpart Alec.

Eddie Campbell is a master cartoonist and has been doing it for decades. He's the illustrator of *From Hell*, if you need to link him up with something more mainstream (which, at the time it was published, wasn't mainstream). I like Eddie's scratchy kind of care-free style and the narratives he brings to the panels is quite intelligent.

I have a few other books by him and have some more in my shopping cart at Amazon.ca

Eddie Campbell is highly recommended if you want to elevate your comics-reading experience.

44.4

One overlooked means to get your name and your book(s)' name out there is to leave reviews and also blurb other authors' books.

On the former: I write a lot of movie reviews. For me, it's my "junk food" writing and something I enjoy doing for fun. Since my main genre of writing is superhero fiction, I write superhero movie reviews (see my book, *Look, Up on the Screen! The Big Book of Superhero Movie Reviews*). I not only post these reviews on my website, but also across the Amazon shopping platforms (.com, .ca, .co.uk). On Amazon, you can decide what your reviewer profile identifies you as. So, simply, you can put your name or a bit of extra info. I put "A.P. Fuchs, author of The Axiom-man Saga." Now, every time someone is scanning the reviews for something I've reviewed, they see my name and my book series. They read my review and it exposes them to my writing style and, hopefully, gets them interested in me and my work.

Reviews also make for great web content for your site because, for example, if you review another author's book and let them know, they might plug your review (thus your site) as they spread the word about it via social media platforms, in turn getting you exposure. Reviews are also a means to get people to keep coming back to your site to see what you review next.

The other thing I mentioned is author blurbs. This is where another writer/creator approaches you and asks you to endorse their book. They usually send you an advance reader's copy. You read it. If you like it, you craft one to two sentences they can use to help promote it. Since it's your blurb, you get the byline so, in my case, if I blurbed a zombie book, my byline would be "A.P. Fuchs, author of the Undead World Trilogy."

As a word of caution, just because someone asks you to blurb their book doesn't mean you should do it in that if indeed the book isn't very good at all, you don't want to have your name attached to it, which is what providing a blurb does. If you run into this situation, you can politely tell the writer that their book wasn't your cup of tea and that you'd rather not provide a blurb at that time.

But if it is good . . .

Then your blurb would be part of either the book's front or back cover, or a praise page within, and also attached to any promo material the author sends out pertaining to that book. Good exposure for you. Gets your name and your work out there.

I've done blurbs in the past. They're fun. I've also written introductions to other people's books, but that's a discussion for another time.

See you all next week.

He is Mysterious. He is Legend. He is Bigfoot. 14 scary stories to satisfy you. BIGFOOT TERROR TALES Vol. 1 http://amzn.to/1xtjlqE

End transmission.

Issue Forty-five - March 14, 2015

It's Friday as I draft this up. Fighting a strange wave of fatigue for the past few days. No matter how much sleep I get, I have that fuzzy fog feeling going on in my head. Hope this newsletter makes sense otherwise just write it off as the ramblings of a tired writer.

Welcome to the new issue.

45.1

This week's writer's rumination:

Was on the phone with a friend the other day and he and I were talking about what TV shows we were each binge watching on Netflix. I mentioned the show the Mrs. and I are watching and, without spoiling it, my friend said the show ends with a lot of unanswered questions, things left up in the air and, apparently, no grand scheme or tightly-woven plot that ties the whole series together. I told him I was fine with that, the reason being that's how life is. We all have our various storylines going on and come the day of our deathbed, we're going to have stuff unresolved or things we won't have the answers to. For me, knowing that a TV show mirrors life in that way is just fine. My friend, on the other hand, likes to have his ducks in a row and for things in his life or have order and make sense.

So after I hung up I got thinking about the idea of why, when it comes to our entertainment—books, movies, comics, plays, etc.—we like for the stories we're presented with to have a complete beginning, middle and end. We like resolution. We like knowing there was a *reason* behind the ups and downs our heroes faced. Case in point, if you're reading a book or watching a movie and suddenly the story just stopped, you'd be pretty upset. You'd want to know the conclusion of what was going on even though deep inside you know that if indeed stories are a mirror of reality, there was no obligation to provide you with one because, again, life is open-ended in a lot of ways.

What drives this? Is it because our lives are indeed open-ended in a lot of respects that when it comes to our fantasy escapes we require the satisfaction of resolution for the stories we vicariously live through? Does being presented with an incomplete tale violate some sort of self-serving notion that we deserve resolution to all conflict?

I spoke to another writer about this because I was genuinely curious why we want our fantasy to work differently than reality. Of course, the short answer is, "Well, it's fantasy. It's *supposed* to be contrary to reality. It's supposed to be good times wrapped in pink ribbons and is supposed to make me feel good while partaking in it."

That doesn't cut it with me. Perhaps because I come from the school of hard knocks, I'm one of those too-bad-so-sad kind of guys. Something doesn't work out or you don't like it? Tough beans. That's life. Get used it. Stop whining.

At the same time, I would be upset if the stories I read/watched didn't have, at the very least, 90% resolution.

My writer friend said the reason people get up in arms about unresolved fictional issues is because as the writer—and this applies to TV or whatever because every story medium has a writer—you are making a promise to the reader to carry them from Point A to Z in full. No Point A to S or A to G, but A to Z. You're promising the reader that whether things work out for your characters or not, you're going to give a coherent picture as to why things are the way they are in that fictional world. If you don't deliver on that, it's a betrayal of trust. Any time a reader embarks on a new book, a certain level of trust is placed in the author to see them through the journey. If the author violates that, he's violated the reader in a manner of speaking because they've pulled the blanket of trust from over them.

I understand this reasoning and it makes sense. I just find it amusing/interesting people need to have their entertainment a certain way or they'll get mad.

What are your thoughts on this? Write in and tell me.

45.2

Keeping current on re-posting the movie reviews to the website.

Wordpress was acting up today so I don't know if it'll correct itself before the day is out so I can do today's update. Regardless, I have around five or six weeks' worth of reviews to post and then I'm all caught up. After that I think I'll do some here-and-there blogging and take a bit of a breather.

Coming to a strange point in my creative career. As each day passes, the more and more I feel like I'm done with the book industry for the time being. I mean, I've been at it since 2000, been publishing since 2003, have written and published over thirty of my own books and have put out over a hundred books for other people. Despite all that being a fairly decent accomplishment, I feel like I'm struggling to make it in this business and each day is a fight. Ironically, I never wanted to be in the book business to begin with. I wanted to make comics. I've already told the story about what happened and why the change so I won't repeat it here, but the point is I'm coming to a place creatively where I want to get back into comics and really make a go of it.

Though this is subject to change, my plan is to finish my upcoming block of book projects then dive headlong into the world of making comics. I won't quit writing novels. I still have *The Axiom-man Saga* to finish, but I will be slowing my literary output in favor of creating stories panel-by-panel.

Just feel like I've accomplished what I've wanted to accomplish book-wise and it's time to move on.

45.3

This week DC Comics released images of Superman's and Wonder Woman's new costumes. Despite me being a fan of the classic Wonder Woman suit, her new look is also beautiful, conservative, and warrior-like. So I'll leave her alone. It's a nice upgrade.

Superman's, on the other hand, is a gong show. I mean, a T-shirt and jeans? Really? I don't mind them changing the S to having a black background, but a buzz cut and no supersuit? Who is this guy? Certainly not the Man of Steel I grew up with.

In an interview with Gene Simmons of KISS, someone once asked him why he and the band wear makeup and costumes? He said why does Superman wear his uniform and not just going around helping people in everyday clothes? Gene said because it wouldn't be Superman, if that was the case and, pertaining to the band, KISS wouldn't be KISS otherwise.

A superhero's costume is more than just some flashy outerwear. It's a symbol of who they are and what they're standing up for. It's meant to be different from regular clothes because a superhero is supposed to stand out from the crowd as a beacon of hope in the dark places of the world. Putting Superman in an everyman outfit robs him of that and does a disservice to all those who look up to him.

I'm very disappointed in DC's move on this part. Hope it's temporary. He doesn't even have a cape.

45.4

As writers, we tend to live in our own little world, not just creatively, but also publishing-wise, too. Whether we publish ourselves or have someone else do it, the mentality is it's me and my books and that's all there is in my little universe.

Here's an idea, and this applies to cartoonists, too:

Sell some short stories to various anthologies, magazines, newspapers, e-zines, etc.

Not only does this mean a few extra bucks in your pocket, but you end up tapping into another publisher's audience as a result. Selling short stories is a good way to showcase your skills as a storyteller, a kind of sampler/resume of your style. Joe Reader reads a tale of yours in an anthology, likes what you did, then seeks out other work by you. Every anthology or magazine has an author bio section—sometimes long, sometimes short—but regardless, this would be the place to plug additional work, where people can find you on the web, where your books are available, etc.

It's also a chance for you to stretch your creative muscles and tell a story in a shorter form instead of something always book-length.

In the end, short stories are a great way to reach new readers and show them what you're capable of. As well, once you've written enough of them, you can always collect them into a book thus adding another title to your bibliography.

For short story markets, aside from keeping your eyes open for submission calls on Facebook or message groups, www.ralan.com is a good place to start. The site's been around for years and lists all sorts of story markets, submission guidelines, compensation, etc.

Well worth looking into.

Know what else is well worth looking into? This:

Bigfoot is back! 16 more terrifying Sasquatch tales in this epic anthology. BIGFOOT TERROR TALES Vol. 2 http://amzn.to/1gdKc3o

End transmission.

Issue Forty-six - March 21, 2015

It would be nice if I could say, "Coming to you live from the desk of A.P. Fuchs" as I write this newsletter, but the reality is it's Thursday as I type this up. When I post it, it'll be Saturday. Not live. In a sense, you're receiving a transmission from the past.

Pseudo-time travel. Yeah, let's run with that.

Welcome, people.

46.1

The more I think about it, the more I believe it.

The book is dead.

I was on the phone the other day with a friend in the business who I talk to roughly once every four to six weeks. I've known him since 2009, I think. He's a good friend and he and I are on the same wavelength for most things publishing/writing-related. This was the same friend who I told you about who had that issue with the artist awhile back.

In January of this year, this friend made a bold move: he pulled all his books—some 150+ of them—from Amazon Kindle. The main reason was he was tired of roughly half of the books regularly coming back as returns, and since book sales aren't what they used to be, it's not like he was cutting off a huge chunk of income even with those returns.

So he drops me a note the other day and asks me to call. I do. He then goes on to tell me that this month—March—he got returns for eBooks on Kindle even though he hasn't had any titles available for sale with them for all of February. Amazon has a 7-day return policy for eBooks. My friend calls them up and talks to the rep on the other end. Turns out Amazon is able to make exceptions for returns outside of that 7-day period at their discretion. I suppose that's fair. Customer service and all that. If you're a few days over the return period, they might still accommodate you.

The day after I talked to my friend, I had to go through my Amazon Kindle sales reports for something. I looked and, sure enough, there was an eBook return. Normally, I don't care. Half my books come back anyway. But then I looked at the title. It was for a book that hasn't been available through my company since over a year ago. Over a year! And this book somehow got returned. I emailed Amazon and told them the situation. Over a year is well outside of their 7-day return policy. They basically told me the same thing they told my friend: they have the ability to award returns based on their own discretion. They said they'd flag the return and investigate why it was returned after so long, but in the end they said there was nothing they can do for me and I'd have to eat the return cost.

I immediately called up my friend and told him what happened. I couldn't believe it.

This made me wonder, then, how many of the returns I get are from outside that 7-day window. Truth is, I'll never know because the sales sheet doesn't tell you when specifically the purchase was made and when specifically it was returned.

Which brings me to my point of the book is dead.

There is no respect for books anymore. Not in the digital age. See, you're not trafficking in books when you publish an eBook. You're trafficking in digital information, something intangible. We live in a world where people want everything for free. Wanna see that latest movie? Go and steal it online. Wanna hear that latest song? Go and download it from a pirate site. Wanna read that book? Go and get it off Kindle, download it to your computer, then return the book.

Free information.

I know people are stealing. I'll get sales for the entire *Axiom-man Saga* all in one go. A few days later, the entire series is returned. Don't tell me you read all seven books in a few days, decided you didn't like them, then wanted your money back. Even the most avid readers don't read books that quickly.

Yet us authors are catering to this by making our books either dirt cheap—99 cents—or even free altogether. If we devalue our work, then why should the reader give it any value, especially when it's just words on a screen and not an actual book?

It's like the dot com boom. Back in the day, if you had a website, you had a lucrative company. Now every Tom, Dick and Harry has a website. They're worthless. Just more data on the information super highway.

Books are turning into that.

To me, printed books—whether novels or graphic novels—are works of art. There's special care taken in not only the creation of the story, but also in how it's presented in the end with the layout, formatting and printing. This is why you find neat books out there with special wrap-around covers, or inserted materials, or pop-up abilities. The packaging of the written word is as important as the words themselves when presenting the book as a final product to the reader. It adds to the experience.

Words on a screen isn't an experience in that regard. It's just data.

And books nowadays are being taken for granted, and Amazon clearly is behind a lot of it. Everyone shouts, "Kindle, Kindle, Kindle," but fail to see that it's completely wrecked the publishing system, has devalued books, and has become an avenue in which to supply cheap entertainment—some good, most bad—in an effort to please the masses. Ah, the chase of the dollar.

Money over art is the mantra these days.

I'm not yet in a position to abandon Kindle. I'm thankful for each sale I get, even if it's only a few. But if Amazon keeps abusing its authors and publishers like this, I have no trouble walking. There are other ways to market my work. I sell as many paperbacks as I do eBooks so I'm not hurting in that regard.

Enough of this. Moving on . . .

46.2

Still working on the layout project. I know, I'm slow. Should have been done by now, but I've gotten a case of the lazies lately and have been doing more putzinig around than actual work. That's okay. I'm fine with taking a break. I have over 30 books behind me never mind the books I published for others, never mind the plethora of novels and short stories I've rewritten for other people (without any credit).

Like I said last newsletter, I'm kinda done with the publishing biz and my goals as a writer. I've done enough. Time to move on to other creative endeavours.

At the same time, even though I plan on getting hardcore into making comics next, writing will still be a part of my life because comics require writing before any drawing anyway.

I love coffee.

46.3

Had a blast this past week going to the comic shop. Normally I go once every month or two and pick up the stuff in my pull box and walk out. This week I was on the hunt for a couple of specific comics. It's honestly been, like, thirteen or fourteen years since I've been looking for a specific title in the back issue bin. Fortunately for me, I found what I was looking for and that was Eddie Campbell's two-issue stint on *Captain America*. So I picked those up along with my usual stuff from my box and also got a couple cheap graphic novels.

Good times.

And just yesterday I ordered up two more graphic novels by two of my favorite comic creators, Noah Van Sciver and Julia Wertz. Those should get here in the next week or two.

46.4

When it comes to marketing your book or comics, when you really boil it down, one of the main objectives is to get your name out there. You want your name to be familiar to people who read and work in your genre(s). At the very least, it's nice to hear when people have heard of you. It's happened to myself. I once heard a story where my name was brought up at Image Comics. I don't know why or who said it, but it's complimenting to know that, in the end, people have heard of me.

Sort of a cheap fame.

There are lots of ways to get your name out there, but here's one that I haven't yet mentioned in this newsletter: commenting on other writers' and readers' blogs.

Most blogs have a comment section beneath each post. If there is a book blog or author or artist's blog(s) that you follow regularly, take the time to comment on what they're posting. It only takes a few sentences from you. You could leave a complimenting note, an opinion, or a simple comment.

Usually, when you do leave a comment, not only does the blog give you the option to leave your name, but it also gives the option to leave a link to your website. Use this.

By regularly leaving remarks on a creator's or industry leader's blog/site, you're notifying the author of that article of your existence as well as those who read the comments section beneath. Become a regular fixture on these blogs and people will start clicking the link to your site, thus exposing them to your work. And, of course, when they find out you are a writer or artist, suddenly your comments carry more weight because you're then viewed as someone who knows what they're talking about because you work in the same industry.

As a caution, don't use the comments section to posts ads and/or blatantly plug your work. You'll be viewed as a spammer and no one will pay attention to you. You might even get called out for it. However, you can slip in phrases like, "As a writer myself . . ." or "When I released my books series, *Such-and-such*, I did this . . ." Things like that. That's subtle marketing. Overt marketing doesn't work on the Web these days anyway.

Last, as a regular commenter on these sites, your name gets familiar to the author/creator who no doubt checks the comments. Somewhere down the line, you might be able to ask them for a favor—i.e. to blurb your book—and since they're familiar with you, you'll have a better chance of them working with you.

There are a gazillion blogs and online publications out there. To comment on every single one on a regular basis would be a full time job on its own. Pick a handful of the most prominent blogs and comment there a few times a week.

Never know what doors will be opened.

Know what door you should open, though? This one:

What happens when someone gives u superpowers but doesn't say what they're for? Find out in AXIOM-MAN http://amzn.to/1khtYfz

End transmission.

Issue Forty-seven - March 28, 2015

Hello, everyone. Welcome back. History has just been expanded by one week. (That's seven days, for those counting.)

If the Apocalypse doesn't happen first, we'll do this again next week, too.

And so . . .

47.1

Been dismayed at the various news stories popping up of Christians saying stupid things. Sometimes the headlines are completely misleading and twist the truth of what went on or who said what. Other times, yeah, a Christian somewhere said something dumb and the media had a field day. Fine. Makes good reading. The part that bugs me about it, since most people believe the media, is it paints Christians with a broad brush and makes us all look like idiots, which isn't the case as I've come across many intelligent Christians over the years. I'd like to think of myself as one, too, but I'll leave that observation up to others to decide.

Anyway, being the loudmouth that I am, I decided to post my thoughts on God in an organized manner on Facebook to the tune of one thought per day. I started Thursday and it'll run for over a week until I'm done. Tune in at www.facebook.com/apfuchs

Some might say this is asking for trouble. Some might find the subject interesting. In the end, I think spirituality is an important thing to discuss because if indeed there is stuff going on beyond what we can perceive with our five senses, then we should be privy to that information in our quest to learn more about ourselves and the universe in which we occupy.

Also on Thursday I celebrated my 10-year wedding anniversary with my wife. We went out for dinner at Chicken Chef with the kids. We're doing another dinner on Saturday with some friends.

These past ten years have flown by. There've been good times and bad, but throughout it all I'm happy to be spending them with my wife.

47.2

Been doing a lot of non-fiction writing this week. There's the construction of this newsletter, and then there was the pre-drafting of my thoughts on God, which I did in MSWord prior to posting on Facebook. I've also been quite lengthy in my replies/comments to the posts to others who have commented on what I've said.

The words flow easily and since this stuff has been circulating in my head for a number of years, it feels good to get them out on paper and look at them as a whole.

Interesting side note: when I stew about a certain topic, no matter how long I hit the replay button in my head, the thoughts and ideas thereof stick around and circulate around my brain. However, I've noticed that when I take the time to dump those thoughts on paper, I'm actually doing just that: dumping them on paper. They seem to leave my head and exist more as a scattered memory than a coherent thought. In order to go back and get the full picture of what I was talking/thinking about, I need to re-read what I wrote.

It's an interesting writing phenomenon and applies to when I do my fiction work as well.

47.3

This week we got to see Jesse Eisenberg revealed as Lex Luthor for the upcoming *Batman v Superman* movie.

It was just headshot, but an interesting reveal. He's bald, which was a worry because there were rumors he wasn't going to be, and he looks intense. He also looks older in the picture than he has in other films, which is important for a guy like Lex Luthor. It's hard to believe a twenty-something would be as powerful as Lex.

What's cool about the picture is if you look closely, you can see Superman reflected in his eyes. Nice touch.

A few weeks back Aquaman was revealed. A while before that Wonder

Woman. With this movie coming up in about year, I think we can start expecting more character reveals in the coming months along with a teaser trailer. I don't know how evenly-paced they have all this planned out, but as the date to premiere draws nearer, the more and more we'll see of this stuff.

47.4

There's an old marketing trick that used to be very popular back when I published my first book and was looking to expand my online presence. This was 2003.

Link exchanges.

It's very simple. You email an author and ask them to link to your website from theirs. In exchange, you'll return the favor.

I remember surfing authors webpages back in the day and checking out the links section on their page. I'd then click on those links to get taken to even more authors' webpages.

What's interesting about this, too, is authors in a particular genre all tended to link up with one another. What this did was make their names commonplace amongst other author's links pages, in turn making readers and other creators more and more familiar with seeing their name.

It's a practice that seems to have fallen by the wayside in the writing world. I don't know why. I see lots of cartoonists linking up and notice the effect of repeatedly seeing the names has on me. But writers? Why did they stop?

I'll admit, I'm still in the process of rebuilding my website since I dismantled it last year and a links page has yet to be put up. But I will put one up. It's good for promoting others and links to pages similar to your own are good for the search engines.

Something to ponder.

You should also ponder picking up this book:

Newly endowed with superpowers, Gabriel must decide what to do with them. See him as Axiom-man in his FIRST NIGHT OUT.
http://amzn.to/1fpeJPv

End transmission

Issue Forty-eight - April 4, 2015

I'm writing to you from Winnipeg, Manitoba, Canada. If you don't know where that is, it's right above North Dakota, USA, near the border, smack dab in the middle of the continent. Sometimes when I think of my city, I view it as a kind of hidey-hole, with so much land being on either side of it in all directions.

It's a good city on the whole. Some call it a big small town. We have around 700,000 people who live here. I often see the same faces when I go out to the store.

It's Good Friday as I write this.

48.1

As I'll mention in 48.2, I've been doing a lot of non-fiction writing this past week. My observation for this first section of the newsletter is this: there shouldn't be a big divide between writing non-fiction and fiction. There used to be, for myself, but not anymore. When I write non-fiction—like this newsletter or an essay or an article—I'm talking with you, the reader, passing on information and telling any stories or giving examples pertaining to the topic at hand. I tend to approach non-fiction writing from a conversational point-of-view as opposed to an academic one. I think it makes the giving—and the receiving—of the information more informal yet just as potent. After all, when we go through our lives and receive information from others, it's often through conversation, whether verbal or via email, social networks or texts.

I've noticed in my fiction writing this same sort of conversational tone. When I sit down to write, I take the coffee shop approach where it's just you and me and I'm telling you about something that happened to a friend of mine. (Except, of course, this "friend(s)" is my character(s).) It gives a playful tone to the narrative without lightening whatever you are trying to convey. It seems to make for easier reading.

One could argue that by taking this approach, I've transferred from being a writer to a storyteller. There's a difference between the two with the latter, in my opinion, being the main goal.

This transition also occurs over time for most writers. When you're first learning and practicing your craft, yes, you are telling a story, but the tone seems more formal and unsure of itself. As the years go by and you find your voice, things change and your recent work reads differently than your earlier efforts. And once you find your voice, telling stories is a breeze because you're speaking as you instead of mimicking another writer(s).

Fiction or non-fiction.

You're just talking.

48.2

Today I wrapped up the first draft of my God presentation that I've been posting to Facebook. All told, it's twelve parts, almost 9,500 words. It'll probably cross that threshold once I revise and add a few things.

Again, you can tune in at www.facebook.com/apfuchs

It's felt good to share my faith. I'm also impressed by the quality of feedback and not once did the threads degenerate into a bunch of arguments as topics like religion tend to turn into. Everyone kept it polite, which is a plus.

If you'd like a copy of the presentation, send me an email and I'll shoot one over to you.

Now that this presentation is over, I hope to get back to fiction writing. Got a book to finish.

48.3

The other day I finally found—at least, I'm 99% sure I found—a book I've been looking for for the past while. It's called *Superfolks* by Robert Mayer. It was published in the '70s and looks at the life of the superhero from the point-of-view of a retired Superman-like figure. What's interesting is the cast of characters are all rip-offs of classic characters (i.e. Captain Marvel, Plastic Man, Mary Marvel and others).

I found out about this novel when reading an interview with Dave Sim, the gist being that if you have a superhero story you want to tell with a popular character but can't convince the rights holders to publish it, then write the story anyway, change the names, add a few minor tweaks to make it "different" and then publish it yourself.

Superfolks took this idea and ran with it. So would've Alan Moore's *1963*, had that project come to fruition.

This idea of "stealing yet making it your own" is different than fan fiction in that, while you might be riffing on an established character, you're at least making enough changes to make it sort of original.

Sort of a gray area of intellectual copyrights.

And, of course, by using your own characters, it can turn into something commercially viable as opposed to fanfic, which is illegal to sell.

48.4

Free eBooks as a means to expand your *paid* readership.

I have mixed feelings on this one so I'll just tell you about my own experience and you can decide for yourself.

A few years ago I released a paranormal romance vampire trilogy. It's out of print now, but wasn't back then. It was released in paperback and eBook. Shortly after release, I made the first installment in the trilogy free as an eBook in the hopes to hook readers into buying parts two and three. Tens of thousands of free copies were downloaded. It's nice to see those kinds of numbers on your spreadsheet. And the few reviews that came in were positive most of the time so I knew the quality of the book was okay.

But you know what?

It didn't help sales of the other two books one bit. There was no noticeable spike. Even if you wanted to play the turn-over game and hope that at least 1% of all those downloads would result in sales in the other books of the series, that never happened.

In the end, my experience with giving a book away for free didn't work out so it wasn't worth it for me other than some exposure, but exposure is useless unless it results in sales.

On the flip side, some authors have had great success giving their books away or selling the first book in a series for .99 cents and then the other installments at regular price.

The sad part about free eBooks is, though you're able to see how many are downloaded, you have no idea how many copies are actually read. Downloads are meaningless without people actually putting their eyes on the story.

My personal feelings toward free books is that they're a waste of time and that by authors putting their stuff out for free, they're further reducing the value of their work in the hopes of being read in a market which is already devaluing the artistic value of a book anyway. Remember, eBooks aren't really books. They're just digital information and are slowly but surely being viewed as "info on the web" versus books people actually put a lot of thought into.

Personally, I think authors should stop the practice of putting work out for free, thus sending a message to the consumer of, "Hey, you want to read this story? You'll have to pay for it. I need to be able to support myself, too." But we won't do that. We're too nearsighted. Need that payoff now.

Hmph, what payoff?

Anyway, my experience. Take it for what it's worth.

As of now, I'm done with giving my work away for free. I don't need the validation of being read as a writer. What I do need is to know that people are interested enough in my stuff that they're willing to shell out a couple of bucks for it. To me, that says they value my work. That's the kind of validation I need.

So, that said, if you'd like to validate me as a writer, please consider this book:

Axiom-man & Redsaw go head-to-head in this superhero thriller & open a doorway to an evil world DOORWAY OF DARKNESS
http://amzn.to/1hMg1o1

End transmission.

Issue Forty-nine - April 11, 2015

Hello,

Was in a time-warp this week. It blew by. Not a fan. I like medium-paced weeks. I think I've said this before. But, time passes. That's the thing with Time. It keeps going whether we want it to or not. As long as you keep going forward, I guess that's all right. Going backward is dangerous. It's tough when your external self moves forward along the timeline but your internal self keeps backtracking. Almost like doing front-and-back splits. Eventually something's going to tear.

Welcome.

49.1

Like all kids, I had to go with Mom and Dad wherever they went when they went out on errands. One day—I was eight or nine—we went to the bank. While my sister and I were waiting for Mom—pretty sure it was Mom—to do her banking, my sister and I went around the whole bank and took a copy of each of the brochures on display. By the time we were done, we had quite a stack. We stuck them in ATM envelopes and took them home. She had hers, I had mine. I sealed the envelopes and to this day they haven't been opened. I took those same packs and, along with a few other important items to me, put them in a box and hid that box as a time capsule in my parents' basement. This was a little over twenty-five years ago. The box had only been opened up once when I had a friend over when I was ten or eleven. Currently the box resides with me, unopened.

Of course, I also created this time capsule when it was brought up at elementary school by one of the teachers and I learned that the cement block with the date of the school's construction actually contained a time capsule in behind it.

Here's the point of the story:

I've written a lot of books. Presently, my personal copies are on a shelf in my studio, those along with other books my stories have appeared in like anthologies and whatnot. A thought I had this week was to take a copy of all my work from my book stock and stick them in a secure box and seal it up for my kids to have and, later, to eventually pass onto their kids and so on down the line.

While these books were originally printed on demand and, at present, I can still print up however many more I need, this might not always be the case, especially with reading becoming more and more electronic.

Will the printed book eventually be phased out? Maybe not in my lifetime but in my kids'? A printed book is not the same as an electronic book, words on a screen. To somehow be able to capture this time in history and seal it away, especially for items as sentimental as books that I wrote, might be a good idea.

Will have noodle with this notion more, but from a family heirloom perspective, it makes sense. Besides, they might be worth a lot of money one day.

Artists tend to be more valued after they're dead.

49.2

Finally finished getting all the pages scanned into the computer for that layout project for a client. It took a while, but I was only picking at it. It's done now. All that's left is to compile the images into a single PDF file and share it with the client for approval. Still working on arranging a time for that.

Also realized this is Issue Forty-nine of *The Canister X Transmission*, which means that after today, there'll be three more issues and then Year One is complete. Which means I'll have another book written as I'll be collecting these issues between two covers. Hard to believe it's been nearly a year already.

Been also thinking about *The Canister X Transmission* Year Two. I want to keep doing the newsletter, but I also don't want it to be same old, same old. People have said they like the four-point format of the current series. And, if you've noticed, these four points have all been thematically the same since we started last May. Should I keep the four points but change up the topics? Should I do a whole new four topics or keep some and lose others? Please email me with your thoughts so I can plan accordingly. I want this newsletter to be for you guys, not just for me.

49.3

We live in a USA-dominated world. Between you, me and the Internet, I think that's partly because they have a way better PR team than other countries. That, and a strong currency. But in terms of world awareness, the USA is very prominent.

As proud as I am of Canada, it often feels like we're playing second fiddle to our southern neighbors.

That said, I'm pleased to report it's not all red, white and blue. I borrowed the complete edition of *Captain Canuck* from a friend and just started getting into it today (Friday). I think I found out about the character some eighteen or twenty years ago or so. How much of a Captain America rip-off he turns out to be, we'll find out as we read. Only read one issue out of the collection thus far.

So far as I know, this collection is also every comic that Captain Canuck has been in. Cumulatively, my own Canadian superhero, Axiom-man, has had more page time than ol' Captain Canuck across the seven books currently released in the series thus far but, of course, isn't nearly as popular. Need to remedy that somehow.

49.4

Following up to last week's bit on offering your eBook for free, this week fellow author Christine Steendam posted about free eBooks on Facebook and her and I got to talking about it since she agrees with me that offering the book for free in an effort to boost sales is a waste of time.

However, she offered the flip side of the argument and that's what I'm going to post here. The flipside is this: using your free eBook to expand and/or boost your author platform, your author platform defined as your online presence, whether that's your Facebook friends, Twitter followers, newsletter sign-ups, etc.

I've seen a few authors—not many, but a few—use Amazon's free Kindle book reach to expand their Facebook and Twitter presence. There's an ad in the eBook which encourages the downloader to follow the author via various social networks.

Then, as I've mention in this newsletter before, there's also using the free eBook as incentive for newsletter sign-up. The more people on your newslist, the better.

I can see the wisdom in going down the platform-building road with free eBooks.

Arguably, webcomic artists use the same tactic, in that they post their comic for free on their website and invite readers to keep in touch via various social media. The downside, of course, is they're giving the product away for free so for that effort in and of itself there is no money to be made. Usually, the webcomic artist then offers print copies of the comic and various other merchandise to make their living.

My personal thought on all of the above is that I can understand how they work in principle but based on what I'm presently seeing/observing and what I know of others' results because of these efforts, it still doesn't seem that effective.

It's all numbers, right? Even if you used your free eBook to build your social media status, it all comes down to active users. For example, 10,000 people download your book. Five percent of them follow you on Facebook, so that's 500 likes. Out of those 500, only a portion is paying attention to what you're doing and out of the portion that is, only a small percentage become future book buyers.

Volume is the key ingredient in the above, I think. The downside is, in publishing, volume is variable X. You never know what's going to hit and what's going to miss, whether that product is free or not.

All I got going on in the back of my noggin is the idea that there must be some sort of happy middle ground. I have no idea what that looks like, but some sort of way for creators to share their work with a truly invested group of people who'll in turn support the creator in question when the time comes. The idea is finding the supporters who are of the mind/knowledge that the creator needs to eat, too, therefore they understand their side of the bargain is shell out a few bucks on that creator to help make that happen instead of sucking up the free resource that is the World Wide Web.

Door's open for thoughts, if you have any.

I'm done for this week. It's 7:45PM Friday night as I type this. I still need to read this thing one time through before shutting down the file. Also need a drink. Maybe a rum and Coke or a beer. We'll see.

Peace out.

Suddenly sucked into a parallel world, Axiom-man finds himself fighting against the ravenous undead in THE DEAD LAND http://amzn.to/hhuLsT

End transmission.

Issue Fifty - April 18, 2015

Fifty issues. Some would consider this cause for an anniversary celebration. The fifty-second issue is the important one, because that marks Year One of *The Canister X Transmission* being complete.

Still, doing this weekly for fifty weeks is nothing to sneeze at. It's also become part of my routine and I don't think a week has gone by where I forgot about it or went, "Uh oh, I got to write the new issue to keep on pace."

So, here we are, seven days since the last one.

50.1

In the interest of shattering any illusion of expertise I might have in your mind, I'd like to inform you that I'm not who you think I am. Sure, I might seem like I know what's going on in the book biz, even know the ins and outs of writing. Granted, knowledge has been gained through experience but I'm really winging this as much as anyone else.

There are two types of writers (same applies to artists): writer-writers, and writers. I'm the latter. A writer-writer is someone who knows all the rules of grammar, the finicky names of each type of word (i.e a past participle; seriously, have no idea what that is). They could tell you how to properly construct a sentence and break it down for you in terms of subject, adjective, etc. They analyze written work looking for themes, style, metaphor and meaning. Words are a big deal to them and writing and books are taken quite seriously.

Which is fine. Just not me.

To be honest, I really don't care about any of this stuff. It's all just fun and games to me and all I'm interested in is telling you a story you might enjoy. Sure, I know how to write properly and when to use what punctuation, but I also break rules all the time. For example, a one-word sentence. See?

I very rarely—perhaps only once or twice—have purposefully put a specific theme into one of my books. I've never written something as commentary to a larger political issue. I've never swam against the current by writing and publishing something that goes against the grain of society just to make a point. I've never gone out of my way to write something brilliant and layered in meaning just to show off what I can do.

I've only written stories that amuse me. If commentary and themes can be extrapolated from them, it's all by accident. It's just stuff that comes out. My main goal with all this is to first entertain myself then entertain you. I'm not interested in writing for the masses or crafting formulaic fiction just to make a buck. I don't want to follow the rules of genre so my work can be marketed a certain way to a certain audience. If anything, such parameters are hindrances to letting a story go where it will.

Which reminds me, writing for an audience or writing to formula is a good way to help boost the chances of success, but that success is only measured in sales. To me, a greater measure of success is writing the book or comic you want to and staying true to your story and your vision. Receiving validation via numerous sales is more just an indicator of marketing versus quality of work.

All depends on your goals. Some people chase after the dollar in this business.

I chase after stories.

I think the human imagination is a beautiful thing and it needs to live and breathe just like you and I do. To follow an idea from conception through to completion in an honest fashion is a big deal and is a chance for the creator to let out what's within themselves without submitting to the confines of a particular market and/or direction.

Come the time I'm laying on my death bed and I'm looking back on my work, I'd rather be happy knowing I told the stories I wanted to tell in the style I wanted to tell them than having bent my creative abilities to another's expectations.

Call me jaded if you want. Sometimes sour grapes are good. They're used to make wine, after all.

My point is simply this: I'm not a writer-writer. Writing is more just a conduit to make my imagination manifest within a budget I can afford (if I had more money, I'd make movies).

50.2

It's Wednesday as I draft up this newsletter. Tomorrow night I'm phone conferencing with the client regarding that layout project I've been yammering on about for several weeks. Tomorrow night we'll determine what additional work/changes needs to be done prior to going to press. (Editor's note: this got bumped.)

In other news, getting my headspace together to complete *Zomtropolis*. The remainder of it has been outlined. Just need to flesh out those scenes and it's done. Once that's done, I'll set it aside and outline the rest of *Mech Apocalypse 2*. Then I'll get *Zomtropolis* ready for publication.

Also need to follow up with the artist about the *Power Jam* books but it keeps slipping my mind. It dawns on me during the day but by the time evening rolls around when the artist is available, I forget. Too lazy to write myself a note.

50.3

The wife and I started watching *Daredevil* on Netflix. We're six episodes in as of this writing. I'm really impressed though the Mrs. has an issue with the gore. I do agree it's a bit gratuitous, but I also realize the show is trying to demonstrate the gruesome reality of street violence. The fight scenes are well done, but last too long, in my opinion, but Hollywood would have nothing to entertain us with if they depicted real fights as they are, that is, usually all it takes is for someone to land a blow or two and it's over.

Storyline-wise, *Daredevil* is strong and there are multiple layers going on especially when dealing with the organized crime aspect of the show. Charlie Cox is a great Matt Murdock and Daredevil. Very human, yet very driven. To me, though, it's Vincent D'Onofrio as Kingpin that's the star. He plays such a good villain, not just in terms of being the bad guy, but also in terms of getting you to sympathize with his character. As of episode six, it comes across Kingpin is trying to do right by the city albeit in a very twisted way. You can see where he's coming from, though, which is what makes it interesting and sets him up nicely as an antagonist to Daredevil.

Hope they renew for a second season.

50.4

The last couple of weeks we've been talking about giving your book away for free as a means to gain readers and sales and have come to the conclusion that it's a waste of time in today's cyber arena. I also hinted at the need for a happy middle ground on this and while I was wandering around outside today, I considered this: audio books.

Years ago—around 2007, I think—podcasting was just beginning and a website called podiobooks.com started. Authors began to record their novels and post them for free at this site for download. If a downloader wanted to donate money as a thank you to the author, they could. No obligation to do so, however.

Here's the point: some of these authors who did this built a sizeable audience for their work, Scott Sigler being a big name in this area. He still releases audio versions of his stuff to this day, but if you want to *read* the book, you have to buy it whether that's in paperback or eBook.

I recorded and released the first *Axiom-man* all those years ago and it's received thousands of downloads in that time. Last year I pulled the audio version completely during my meltdown, but I've been thinking of releasing it again.

I'm curious if this audio thing might be a means to grow your audience while still maintaining the need to pay for the written version of the book? Sure, some people would download because they're audio fans and that's how they "read" their books. On the flip side, others might download it, enjoy it, then want a copy for their collection.

Creating a free audio version also combats written piracy in that it's a lot harder for someone to make a plagiarized copy of your book from an audio file versus buying your eBook, putting a new name on it and a new cover, then selling it as their own (and, yes, this does happen; another downside to the whole eBook thing).

They'd have to get voice-to-type software, translate it then check it to make sure the translation worked. Too much work for the lazy thief.

It also makes you as the creator a more versatile entertainer because you're bringing your work to market in an easy-to-absorb format: sound.

Something I've been thinking about as I think the future of fiction creativity lies in a multi-faceted/multi-presented approach where the creator becomes his/her own studio that broadcasts the entertainment they create.

Monetizing it, on the other hand, is always the trick but roping people in via audio sampling/full listening might be a good method.

After all, we need to do something to compete for the attention of those who'd rather watch TV or play videogames.

And so . . .

The city is covered in a black cloud and a new supervillain has taken over. Axiom-man battles it out in CITY OF RUIN http://amzn.to/1gxybUM

End transmission.

Issue Fifty-one - April 25, 2015

Today is Tuesday for me. It's Tuesday for a lot of other people, too.

Got inspired last night about this week's and next's newsletters so jotted down some notes as to what I wanted to cover.

Hope everyone is well.

Amendment to last week's issue: my wife pointed out some misreporting on my part. She's right. I'm wrong. (The story of my marriage.) Here's the correction: I was wrong when I stated that I haven't ever written to market. This was incorrect in three respects: 1) I have written specific anthology stories when asked and 2) a long while back I wrote a trilogy of novellas entitled *Blood of my World*, which were vampire romance novellas. I wanted to see if they would make me a quick buck and if indeed writing sell-out fiction was profitable. Turns out it wasn't, and they were released at a time before the market was flooded with the same nonsense. I made a few dollars, but nothing life-changing. My other books sold more. Last, 3) I wrote some zombie fiction which, for a time, was profitable.

Goes to show how bad my memory is. At least I was accurate in reporting that I no longer write to market. Don't have the patience for it and if releasing different titles in different genres over the years has taught me anything, it's confirmed time and time again that publishing is a giant crapshoot and there's no telling what'll hit. All you can do is keep writing and publishing and hope for the best.

Excuse me while I wipe the egg off my face.

51.1

In the interest of being a grouch, it's easy to get tired and/or burnt out creatively. You can only keep the fire stoked for so long before things start to cool. So the question is, what do you do? Do you let it fizzle and, eventually, walk away? Or do you try and stir up the flames?

The latter, of course.

Here's how I do it:

When I'm feeling creatively drained or just plain tired with this business, I look to my fellow writers and artists for inspiration. I'll either talk to them directly, or read their blogs, their newsletters, their Facebook posts and Tweets. I find that reading about their everyday lives and also whatever creative tidbits they put forth gets me jazzed up again and motivated to keep going. I suppose it has to do with knowing I'm not alone in being human. Having kind of lived my life as someone/thing of an island, it's easy to get swept up in the notion that you're the only one struggling with the day-to-day or having an issue getting thoughts on paper. To discover other creative types go through the same thing is immensely encouraging.

See, when I started creating circa 1994 or 1995, I always thought of career artists as living on some kind of higher plain of existence. After all, they had made it and had their act together. Whether they were full time comic artists or writers, I always looked up to them as celebrities. As the years went by and I got to know people in the business, I learned that they were just as human as I was. They had families, money issues, sick days, frustration, etc. Even the movie stars I've met over the years and have talked to at length have shown me their humanity. They're no longer "up there" but are down here with me.

This idea of inspiring other creative people is one of the reasons I'm so honest in these newsletters. I want to inform those reading them that they're not alone in the good times or bad times of the business. I want to tell them that I get it and that I'm human, too, and, hopefully, provide some encouragement along the way.

So look to your peers. Read up on what they're doing. Get talking to them.

Get inspired.

51.2

Talked yesterday with the client regarding that book layout project. We went over everything and I made a list of changes that needed to be made. The good part was this person was very happy with what I did and the required changes are minor.

On a tougher note, I just got slammed with a heap of administrative work to do for this business. It was work I had originally hired out—*twice!*—and the assigned task had not been delivered on. Looks like I have no choice but to do it myself, which means that it's taken a little over a year for me to come back to square one. That means this work could have been completed a year ago instead of dealing with others to get it done for me. I'm hurt and upset over how this has gone down. Good part is I'm not out any money because I don't pay for services not rendered.

Let this be a lesson to you: be careful who you work with. You need to be sure that whomever you hire for whatever task is trustworthy and dependable. Don't just hire anybody. Do your research into that person, get a history, then make a decision.

This new onslaught of work has derailed my writing plans for the next few weeks, which sucks because I have a bunch of projects in various stages of development that I want to see through to the finish line.

51.3

Last week the *Batman v Superman* teaser trailer was released.

Finally.

I've been obsessively following this movie since it was announced. (Even watched the leaked trailer before the official one debuted.)

Simply put: the movie looks amazing.

I admit, after watching it, I was a bit underwhelmed but I don't know if that had to do with the actual trailer or with me being so hyped up for it that I was expecting my mind to be blown off a simple teaser. After watching it several times, I realized that this flick is a direct continuation of *Man of Steel* and is set to explore Superman's place in the world from a realistic point-of-view. I think that is one of the strengths of this new DC movieverse: it's real. *Man of Steel* demonstrated that and despite what you might have thought of that movie, here's my argument for how real it was: there was a public outcry from moviegoers over all the destruction in it. Why would this be? We've seen Superman bulldoze a city in the comics, in the cartoons. Why did showing him do that in "real life" suddenly hit a nerve? Because actually showing Superman in his true power scared people because we've never seen his power displayed in live action before. The "super feats" of all previous movies and TV were child's play compared to what was depicted in *Man of Steel.* Suddenly, we saw humans weren't the most powerful species on the planet.

This feeds into the storyline as suggested by the *Batman v Superman* teaser. It also seems it's one of the reasons Batman goes to investigate Superman. It also sets up Lex Luthor to not trust the Man of Steel.

Superman himself Henry Cavill says it's not a direct *Man of Steel* sequel, but it seems sequel-ish enough to carry over elements from 2013's Superman outing.

Visually, the flick looks dark. I don't mind darkness and grit, but I suspect that won't be the tone of the overall film. It seems the scenes presented were Gotham scenes and if you know Gotham from the comics and cartoons, it's a very gloomy place. I suspect the Metropolis scenes will be much brighter.

Nothing was shown or mentioned of Wonder Woman or Aquaman in the teaser, which is good. I'm sure Wonder Woman will show up in a future one, but I think Aquaman will be saved for the film itself as he'll probably just have a small scene somewhere toward the end.

Anyway, so far so good. I'm excited to see more footage as we get closer and closer to release.

51.4

There was a time when I recommended LinkedIn as a good network for marketing your book. This was back when it was new. The network has changed as time went on and is now more of a resume network versus a social one. Which is fine, because there is a place in today's job market for such a network. (i.e. when you apply for some jobs nowadays, you have the option to give your LinkedIn link.)

For the writer or artist, LinkedIn isn't a place to sell your books or comics. You can certainly link to your website and all the rest and point people to it, but in terms of advertising your book or comic, that's not what LinkedIn is for. LinkedIn is for marketing *you* in terms of your skills and abilities.

This is a good thing for writers and artists because you can put forth your skills on your LinkedIn profile and also back them up by way of accomplishments (i.e. author of over 30 books in various genres). When it comes time for a publisher or editor—or even another writer or artist—who needs to work with someone with your skillset, your LinkedIn profile is your resume to show them what you can do. This is good for getting hired to write stories or do book covers or whatever.

Likewise, some publishing markets are more formal than others so to include your professional LinkedIn profile as part of your query letter, it's like handing out a digital version of your resume when trying to sell yourself as a writer or artist.

In summary, LinkedIn is a good place to sell *you*, but not for selling your books. However, you might make some book sales by proxy if people are impressed by what they read on your profile.

Speaking of selling oneself, I'm available for appearances worldwide. Just pay my airfare and hotel, and give me a shrimp dinner.

On a serious note, I'm going to sell you this:

What happens when a young girl versed in kung fu takes Axiom-man on a jaunt throughout the city? UNDERGROUND CRUSADE. http://amzn.to/1m0aHL5

End transmission.

Issue Fifty-two - May 2, 2015

Welcome to the end of a one-year journey here at *The Canister X Transmission.*

The first issue launched May 10, 2014 and each Saturday a new issue went out. A couple times it went out Friday or Sunday due to events beyond my control, but regardless, we've been at this for a year so raise your glasses and thank you for coming along for the ride.

As a special thank you for keeping up with me, this fifty-second issue is going to be a double feature, so eight bullet points instead of four. As I'm writing this late Tuesday afternoon, I only have ideas for the first half so we'll see where the muse takes me.

Most importantly, I'm just glad you've stuck around. We've only lost one subscriber throughout the whole year, which makes me feel good about this newsletter as a whole.

Let's get started.

52.1

To commemorate one year's worth of issues, I thought I'd give you an idea of how this newsletter started.

Years ago, I was fascinated by the newsletter concept thanks to Piers Anthony and Darrell Bain. These guys did a monthly newsletter on their website. At the time, it appealed to me for two reasons: 1) having a regular monthly publication and 2) the idea of possibly only needing to blog once a month. Given that my workload was ridiculous at the time, the latter was an attractive option. But I have a hard time shutting up and so decided to both blog *and* run a newsletter. The first *Canister X Newsletter* (I think that was the name) lasted five monthly issues. Then it became a chore to do it and so was abandoned. It also wasn't quite *me.* I released it via a downloadable PDF document.

But I still liked the newsletter concept despite my own failings so kept checking in with Piers and others throughout the years. I also subscribed to a couple of other authors' email newsletters but they were pretty much just promo emails showcasing that author's book(s). That's fine from a simple advertising point-of-view, but there was a disconnect between myself and those authors for that reason. It was just ads.

Along comes Warren Ellis a couple years back with *Orbital Operations*, his weekly newsletter which I get on Sundays. As an Ellis fan, I subscribed and started reading the issues when they came out. This was a newsletter unlike any I had seen as a lot of it was a kind of info dumping ground for Warren's brain. This got me thinking about all the extra crap I got going on in my head and my urge to write it all down, but yet what was the use of writing it all down if there was no one to share it with? At best it'd just be an exercise in catharsis.

For a week or three, I thought about my own newsletter and how I wanted something akin to Warren's but at the same time something I could call my own, thus the rebirth of *The Canister X Newsletter*, but this time with a new name: *The Canister X Transmission*. It'd be a chance to start fresh, get some new ideas onto the virtual page and share them with those who were interested. I put my notice on my website and social media and advertised it. For that first issue, it went out to all of four people. Thankfully, as the year progressed, the list has grown like crazy and I'm encouraged to know there's a sizeable audience out there who's open to hearing from me week-to-week.

Anyway, like I was saying, I wanted my newsletter to be my own thing so I took a cue from Dan Hon's newsletter in terms of the bullet point layout and settled on four main things I'd like to talk about every week after a bit of an intro. For the past 52 weeks, we've led off with a writing/creative thought/musing of the week, followed by a work/project update, then some fanboy news, and lastly, the publishing/marketing tip of the week. It's my hope that my goal of making these four points speak to both writers *and* artists succeeded. If I dropped the ball somewhere along the way, I apologize.

So that's this week's writing thought: this newsletter and how it started.

As of this writing, I'm not one hundred percent on Year Two's plan in terms of what I'm going to cover. A lot of people told me they like the newsletter just as it is, but at the same time I'd like to do something new with it.

I guess we'll find out next week, won't we?

52.2

Work-wise, things are pretty much where they were last week so I'll spare you the details. However, I thought it'd be fun to give a behind-the-scenes look at my tools of the trade since every writer works a bit differently than others. I'll also give you a brief history of the tools I've used over the years.

Rewind to 2000. I was in my apartment. Suddenly, something turns on inside of me and I decide I want to be a writer. That same night, I went into my kitchen where my 386sx IBM desktop was set up and started writing a story. All I remember was that it was about an angel fighting some demons.

That story is now lost. No idea where it is.

Later on in 2000 I moved back in with my folks. Once back home, I still plunked away on that old computer, writing comic scripts and a short story. My dad had bought a Mac while I was still in high school and since the Mac ran faster than my old PC, I started using it instead. It was on that computer where I worked on a series of short stories that would all tie together. As I was working on it, I realized the story was way bigger than I originally planned so these short stories became the beginnings of my first novel, *A Stranger Dead.*

Time went on and I finished my book.

I also wrote a lot of poetry during this time and walked around with a small notebook in my pocket, both for poems and for story ideas. While I no longer write poetry—just not inspired to—I still get plenty of ideas but have now adhered to what [I think] Stephen King said about ideas. He basically said if it's a good one, it'll stick around. If it's bad, you'll forget about it. So these days it's all mental logging for me.

Back to the past.

When it came time to write my second book, I was inspired by Stephen King, who wrote *Dreamcatcher* longhand. Wanting to imitate him, I decided I'd write my second book in a notebook. I did mine in a binder filled with looseleaf, both at home and in the coffee shop. I finished the book in roughly three months (I think). Then came the task of typing it up, which took me eight months because I hated doing it so much. I typed it up on my old PC, the 386sx. (This book was eventually sent to an editor who destroyed it with red ink, but it was the greatest writing lesson I've ever received. So far, this book has never been published.)

My next book, *April*, was written on my parents' Mac. The Mac was good for word processing, but when it came time for me to submit the novel around—and just like with *A Stranger Dead*—I had to use my brother's PC to convert the files to a PC-recognized format. This was before these systems were compatible file format-wise.

I started my fourth book, *A Red Dark Night*, on a PC at my day job. I wrote the opening scene there. I finished it on a brand new Acer PC I bought and had in my room at home. It was on this computer that Coscom Entertainment started and it was this same computer that I used for multiple books all the way up until *Axiom-man: The Dead Land* (I think).

Side note: All PC work was done in Microsoft Word or MSWorks. On occasion, I would type up something in Notepad but it'd still wind up in Microsoft Word at the end.

Like all technology, things got old and I was having a hard time sitting down at the desk and writing. I just wasn't comfortable. It was also around this time my wife and I moved into our house and I had lots more space to work in as opposed to our apartment. Often I'd be sitting on the couch wanting to write, but that would mean I'd have to get up, go up three floors to my studio, wait for the computer to boot up, then get down to work. By the time all that happened, the muse had left and it was hard to get the words out.

It was also around this time that the Acer I was working on was slowing down memory- and speed-wise and I needed something more powerful. By this time the Acer was around six or seven years old. In computer time, that's eons.

Having some extra cash at the time, the Mrs. and I went out to the store and did some computer shopping. We came away with not only a brand new top-of-the-line desktop PC, but also a fairly powerful laptop. (Both Hewlett-Packards.) It was the laptop that was the bigger deal to me because that meant I could write wherever I wanted in the house and didn't have to sit at a clunky desk. I wrote many novels on that laptop. Some on the couch in the rec room, others in my bed, others on the couch in the front room—it was great.

That brings us up to date. When it comes to writing novels, I write them on the laptop in whatever location I feel comfortable in. Non-fiction books are written on the desktop for some reason. I think it has to do with headspace and when I'm doing non-fiction, I'm just talking so can write that wherever because I don't have to think too hard about it. When it comes to fiction, I need to be in the zone thus the laptop's portability makes that possible.

For writing comics, however, though I've done scripts on the desktop, I find writing them longhand in a notebook works best for me. Something about both the portability—I wrote the majority of the *Fox* graphic novel in the coffee shop—and using a pen seems to help with comic creativity.

When it comes to editing, I've always been a printout guy. When I first started editing my manuscripts, I used a red pen because, I think, Stephen King used a red pen. Then I realized years later that a pen is a pen and now I just take whatever pen is available regardless of color and use that to mark up my manuscript.

Once I've gone through my manuscript, I'll sit down at the desktop PC and type up my edits. It's my least favorite thing to do out of the entire creative process but is a necessary evil. And I do it on the desktop PC because it's on the desktop where I take that laptop manuscript and start feeding into the production line to turn it into an actual book.

For my publishing process, please see my how-to book, *Getting Down and Digital: How to Self-publish Your Book* (http://amzn.to/1eBljN5).

52.3

Ever since I was a kid I've been collecting something. My first official collection was hockey cards. Still have them. I was super careful to keep each card as mint as possible and store them in those binder sleeves, with the very important and/or rare cards in hard plastic sleeves.

When I bought action figures, I not only inspected the card, I also inspected the figure itself and its paintjob to make sure the figure I bought was as pristine as possible. I was even careful when putting them in the grocery bag when leaving the store so as to not accidentally bend the card.

Later, when I got into collecting comics, I bagged and boarded each issue right after getting them from the shop. I'd take them out to read, of course, but then they'd go right back into the bag/board and into the comic box. I bagged and boarded them because I'm a collector-reader and am particular about keeping my stuff in as good condition as possible. Even with my paperbacks and hardcovers, I'm extra careful. I'll never break the spine on a paperback and when I read a hardcover, I always have the dust jacket off until I'm done reading it.

I've been reading/collecting this way for about twenty years.

Enter my kids. They've gotten more heavily into comics lately despite having me buy the occasional one for them since as soon as they could read. My oldest is like me: he bags and boards every issue and is careful when he reads them. He's almost ten. My youngest gets his comics from the shop bagged and boarded—since they're usually back issues—and immediately upon getting home, he pulls them out and leaves them out. He's seven and a half. I asked him repeatedly if he wanted to keep his comics safe in bags and boards. Nope. He doesn't care. He just wants to read them and leaves them lying around loose when done.

There's a lesson here and one especially geared for a guy like me who can be so particular about his collection: at the end of the day, the stuff on the pages are just stories. That's all it is. Whether comics or books, it's just stories and unless you have plans to sell off your collection one day, it really doesn't matter what condition they're in because what matters most is the enjoyment you get out of them. Likewise, you can't take them with you when you die.

Of course, I'm not saying don't take care of your stuff. Just saying to put things into perspective. It's easy to obsess over the small items, especially in the context of collecting. After all, the better condition something is in, the more monetary value it has. And yet, that monetary value is useless if you never plan on selling your stuff and want to keep it in the family.

Nowadays, if I get a ding in one of my books or something happens to a comic page, I don't care. I'm not selling them. They're for me and my kids to enjoy. (Though, I will admit, I'm still careful when lending books and comics to the kids since they're at the age where they're still learning to take care of stuff.)

My dad once told me that I'd end up learning more from my kids than I would ever teach them. The above is just an example of that. I've also seen that statement come true in other ways the longer I've been a parent.

Anyway, yeah. They're just stories. Let it go. Have some fun. Be responsible but don't get crazy about it.

52.4

Bruce Lee was arguably one of the greatest martial artists of all time. He achieved this through hard work and an insatiable appetite for martial knowledge. He read everything on martial arts and it's said his personal library was some 2000 books' worth. He also had a philosophy of application which was basically the idea of adopting/keeping what works and discarding what doesn't.

This applies to the writer and artist.

I recommend viewing your publishing and/or creative endeavor as a kind of laboratory. There isn't one set method to doing things. Much of it is finding what works for you and running with it.

Here's how you go about doing that:

Pay attention to what other creators are doing, both in terms of how they create, but also in how they publish and get their work out there.

Read up on publishing and marketing techniques as much as you can. Learn from those who are successful at what they do and try out their methods. I say "try out" because what works for me might not work for you, but you won't know that until you try. I suggest practicing techniques and ideas for a set amount of time—length will depend on the size/scope of the idea—and see if it works for you and yields results, whether that's in sales or networking or exposure, or whether that method's yielded a quality product in the end. If it does the job, good, keep it. If it doesn't, then at least you tried it and can cross it off the list.

Looking back over my career, the way I run things now is much different than how I did back at the beginning. Things have changed so much that I've had to adapt to new technologies and platforms along the way. I've also spent countless hours studying what other authors and artists are doing not only in terms of what they're producing but also in how they're getting it out there. I've tried doing what others have done. Some stuff worked, some stuff didn't. Now I know.

Of course, the idea of *trying everything* can be daunting and by no means am I suggesting to suddenly attempt handling three hundred production and marketing ideas at once. What I am saying is to be willing to be versatile with your current setup and not be afraid to try a method of publishing or marketing that you haven't yet done before.

It's easy to live in our own little creative bubble and be set in our ways in terms of our processes. It's easy to block people or methods out. But publishing is an ever-evolving business and what works today might not work tomorrow. You need to be willing to experiment. You need to be willing to take the time to study the creators you admire and see what they're doing in terms of product offering, publication method(s), distribution, marketing, etc.

Take notes. Make a list of stuff that jumps out at you, then start incorporating those items into your own platform. Keep what works, discard what doesn't.

Hone your skills. Build your knowledge.

52.5

I admit to being a bit of a curmudgeon when it comes to technology, the Internet specifically. I wasn't exposed to the Web until 1996, and back then it was pretty much a place for a bit of research and some email. It wasn't until I started writing that the Web became a critical tool for my career. And, to be honest, I could pretty much do without it if it wasn't for my career as a writer. The Net's about communication, right, and so is writing. They go hand-in-hand.

But that's not what I want to talk about. The thing that is concerning to me is how dependent we are on the Internet. And you have to remember, the Internet is more than just Facebook or email. Not only is it a place of entertainment and knowledge, it's also a place of commerce and many businesses achieve a great deal of revenue from their on-line stores. Even companies that function primarily off-line are Internet-dependent because that's how the company keeps running it's day-to-day (i.e. file sending, interoffice and extra-office emails, memos, texts, records, dealing with other companies, etc.).

It's all computers and information these days, and while having such technology has made our life easier in a lot of ways and has grown us as a species, I'm finding it is also dangerous the more and more tech-dependent we get. I mean, look at your day. How much of it is spent plugged in, whether that's on your phone, your computer, you tablet, your TV? Even TVs nowadays are plugged into the Web.

There seems to be a very real intertwinement of man and technology, so much so that we're now blending man and machine in various ways, whether that's Google's glasses or bionic limbs for amputees, the new Apple watch coming out, RIFD chips and more. In other words, technology is growing and becoming more and more integral to our lives.

My question—and point of this—is simply: what would happen to the world if you suddenly took that all away?

We'd fall apart.

We're no longer a self-sustainable species. We have one foot holding us up via our physical capabilities, the other foot planted in the digital world to keep us balanced. Imagine one day waking up suddenly having to do everything while standing on one leg?

The majority of our infrastructure of our society is based on computers and the Internet. We get hit by an EMP, it's all over. Chaos everywhere.

This shows me that we're not as great as we think we are. We think that since we have all this tech we're suddenly these great achievers. What we're actually doing is creating dependency and disabling ourselves from making it on our own like our ancestors did.

The world got on just fine without digital technology and, before that, industrial technology. People back then relied primarily on themselves to get day-to-day living done. Drop someone off from 2015 back in the 1600s and that person would have a real problem.

I worry for the day when our tech is suddenly swept out from under our feet.

52.6

Because I don't mention it enough, I want to remind you of where I am on the Web. If we haven't hooked up via these avenues, then by all means, please do. Likewise, this newsletter is meant for sharing so please tell others about it and give them the link below.

Website roundup:

Newsletter: www.tinyletter.com/apfuchs
Main hub: www.canisterx.com
FB: www.facebook.com/apfuchsbooks
Twitter: www.twitter.com/ap_fuchs
Pinterest: www.pinterest.com/apfuchs
Email: coscomentertainment@gmail.com

52.7

Social media is a weird machine and in general it serves one purpose: to socialize, just as the name implies. However, it also serves as a broadcast point for individuals and businesses to get their message out there, their message being more than just, "How're you doing?"

For your regular user, social media is mainly used for socializing and sharing info, but when it comes to the author or artist—namely because, technically, we're in showbiz—our social media serves that dual purpose: socialization and broadcasting. We tell others about our books and update on what we're working on while also conducting the mundane of everyday conversation.

A trap that can easily be fallen into—and I've fallen into it myself—is the idea that our social media audience is out there hanging on our every word, anxious for our next post. I don't mean to be the bearer of bad news but this is vain thinking and is basically the product of an ego trip. While it's true that in some cases, yes, we can't wait to hear from our favorite celebrity (regardless of field), on the whole, average creative Joes like you and me, well, no one could give two rats' tails about us. I mean, the Internet will go on if we miss a day of posting.

I point out this fault in thinking because, like I said, I've fallen into the trap of thinking people on my social media feeds are out there just waiting for my next post and, secondly, the notion that people are out there waiting for us only further binds us to the technology that I ranted about in section 52.5.

There is such a thing as the "less is more" principle and for social media, I think there's a lot of truth in that. I'm more apt to find it special when someone tweets or FB posts now and then versus all the time, and I've come across both. It seems to carry more weight because, usually, those who post now and then post something of value versus "my feet are sore." I'll tell ya, the all-the-time stuff is a pain. I don't care what color your shirt is or what your dog is doing. However, I do care when you say something witty or clever, or share something uplifting or offer some constructive advice. I even still care if you want to tell me about your latest project. Just don't beat me over the head with it.

All I'm saying is if the above is you, that is, you think you're God's gift to the Internet (okay, that's a bit extreme but you know what I mean), then maybe it's time to re-evaluate where you stand on the celebrity hierarchy. And, frankly, even if you're at the top, I don't need to know what's going on every minute of your life. I got my own that's busy enough.

52.8

Ever since I was a little kid, I've always been fascinated by the battle between Good and Evil. It was birthed in my love for superheroes and the concept of Good vs Evil has been a consistent theme throughout my entire life. The struggle is all around us. I mean, just look at the headlines. Look at your own life, your own issues, trials and temptations.

Once I was old enough to be told about the *true* battle between Good and Evil going on behind-the-scenes—angels vs demons and, ultimately, Christ versus Satan—my fascination with the subject grew even more. Really, we're talking about extreme superheroes versus extreme supervillains, and now and then this war spills into our reality. (I know many stories of people actually seeing this stuff never mind my own personal experience with it.)

That said, this is one area of my Christian study that I've been getting more and more into. No, I'm not going to preach to you. Just going to share some things.

The world of angels and demons is more than just a couple chubby cherubs fighting some ugly bat-like critters with a flimsy bow and arrow. Angels are powerful figures who put Superman to shame any day of the week. They're skilled warriors, tacticians and also ministers and messengers. Fallen angels, however, are extremely dangerous. They are powerful as well and are very cunning. They even appear as the good guys sometimes to dupe you into believing them.

Both sides have a chain of command and there are different types of angels and demons, not just one variety. Each has a function that serves a greater whole like our own militaries do.

As a researcher into the field of angels and the supernatural, a person needs to be careful because you want to make sure that what you're learning about them is indeed correct about how they function. For the angel side of things, the Bible's the best place, same for demons. However, if you get into reading extracurricular material—especially any dark material—you want to make sure you don't accidentally open any doors to things you'd rather not deal with. (I have a friend who fooled around with the Necronomicon and the stuff that went down as a result is crazy scary.)

Hope I haven't weirded you out, but the supernatural is an incredible field of study and one that is slowly becoming more and more taboo in our science/tech-based society. Perhaps it's its "forbiddingness" that makes it appealing?

Again, tread with caution.

All right, this double issue is now concluded. Thanks again for tuning in for the past 52 weeks. Next week we start Year Two of *The Canister X Transmission.*

All back issues are available at www.tinyletter.com/apfuchs and soon they will be collected in trade paperback and eBook formats if you'd like to have a copy for your shelf.

This year I transmitted to you a little over 65,000 words.

Ad:

End transmission.

About the Author

A.P. Fuchs is the author of many novels and short stories. His most recent books are *Mech Apocalypse, Axiom-man: Outlaw; Axiom-man: Episode No. 2: Underground Crusade; Getting Down and Digital: How to Self-publish Your Book; Look, Up on the Screen! The Big Book of Superhero Movie Reviews*; *Canadian Scribbler: Collected Letters of an Underground Writer.*

Also a cartoonist, he is known for his superhero series, *The Axiom-man Saga*, both in novel and comic book format.

Fuchs's main website is **www.canisterx.com**

www.ingramcontent.com/pod-product-compliance
Lightning Source LLC
Chambersburg PA
CBHW061552210726
48287CB00006B/2155

* 9 7 8 1 9 2 7 3 3 9 5 5 8 *